DATE DUE

STUDIES IN ROMANCE LANGUAGES: 14

DRAMA & ETHOS

Natural-Law Ethics
in Spanish Golden Age Theater

Robert L. Fiore

THE UNIVERSITY PRESS OF KENTUCKY

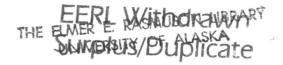

ISBN: 0-8131-1327-X

Library of Congress Catalog Card Number: 74-18931

Copyright © 1975 by The University Press of Kentucky

A statewide cooperative scholarly publishing agency
serving Berea College, Centre College of Kentucky,
Eastern Kentucky University, Georgetown College,
Kentucky Historical Society, Kentucky State University,
Morehead State University, Murray State University,
Northern Kentucky State College, Transylvania University,
University of Kentucky, University of Louisville, and
Western Kentucky University.

Editorial and Sales Offices: Lexington, Kentucky 40506

for Jannette, David, & Gabriella

Contents

". . . the imitation, which is also an action, must be carried on by agents, the *dramatis personae*. And these agents must necessarily be endowed by the poet with certain distinctive qualities both of Moral Character (*ethos*) and Intellect (*dianoia*)—one might say, of heart and head; for it is from a man's moral bent, and from the way in which he reasons, that we are led to ascribe goodness or badness, success or failure, to his acts. Thus, as there are two natural causes, moral bent and thought, of the particular deeds of men, so there are the same two natural causes of their success or failure in life. And the tragic poet must take cognizance of this."

Aristotle

Acknowledgments

Many of my colleagues and friends have contributed in various ways toward the completion of this study, and it is my sincere pleasure to acknowledge their assistance and encouragement.

I should especially like to record my gratitude to the late Cyril A. Jones of Oxford for his many valuable suggestions. The great profit I have derived from discussions with him on the problems raised by the interpretation of Calderón is, I hope, faithfully reflected in my book. To William C. McCrary of the University of Kentucky, who set so high a scholarly example for me, and George Mansour of Michigan State University, I am indebted for their thoughtful reading of the manuscript, constructive suggestions, and sound advice. Robert Lucas of the University of North Carolina at Chapel Hill, the late Charles D. Blend of Michigan State University, and John E. Keller of the University of Kentucky have my deep appreciation for their helpful criticism, interest, and encouragement.

Michigan State University granted a summer stipend which permitted me to complete the final draft of this work. Typing, photocopying, and other clerical assistance were subsidized by All-University Research Grants from Michigan State University. Mr. Leslie Scott and the Michigan State University Development Fund helped financially with publication.

The editors of *Hispanic Review* and *Hispania* have generously granted me permission to incorporate in revised form my articles "*El gran teatro del mundo:* An Ethical View," *Hispanic Review* 40 (1972), and "Natural Law in the Central Ideological Theme of *Fuenteovejuna,*" *Hispania* 49 (1966).

Finally, to my wife Jannette, I express my deepest appreciation not only for her wise suggestions but even more for her patience, tolerance, and encouragement.

Chapter One

The Climate of Opinion
in Golden Age Spain

Thomistic natural-law ethics, the most important element of the revival of Scholasticism in Golden Age Spain, was extremely influential in the intellectual climate of this period, impressing itself upon many areas of Spanish thought. Scholars have demonstrated the importance of natural law with relation to the political thought of Counter-Reformation Spain, yet despite its pervasive influence on the literature of the period, no major studies have treated this topic. The impact of the notion of natural law on Golden Age literature can best be seen in the drama, where philosophical tenets are often essential to theme. Given the fact that natural law is such an important aspect of the literature of the Golden Age, it is helpful for the literary student to have a knowledge both of this philosophical doctrine and of the cultural climate in which it flourished.

Carl L. Becker traces the relationship of natural philosophy, and specifically of Thomistic natural law, to the climates of opinion prevailing in different periods of history. Having stated Aquinas's definition of natural law and Dante's arguments for a world monarchy, Becker relates these to the concept of climate of opinion.

Professor Whitehead has recently restored to circulation a seventeenth-century phrase—"climate of opinion." The phrase is much needed. Whether arguments command assent or not depends less upon the logic that conveys them than upon the climate of opinion in which they are sustained. What renders Dante's argument or St. Thomas' definition meaningless to us is not bad logic or want of intelligence, but the medieval climate of opinion—those instinctively held preconceptions in the broad sense, that *Weltanschauung* or world pattern—which imposed upon Dante and St. Thomas a peculiar use of the intelligence and a special type of logic. To understand why we cannot easily follow Dante or St. Thomas it is necessary to understand (as well as may be) the nature of this climate of opinion.[1]

Spain's climate of opinion had changed a great deal during the course of the Renaissance, and by the end of the sixteenth century the dominant theological and philosophical views had reverted to some extent to those held during the Middle Ages. One popular concept common to these periods was that God guided man to his ultimate end; artists preferred to express this idea metaphorically, representing God as Dramatist and the world as a great theater.[2] Man accepted his role in the drama with resignation, since he could not alter the divine text; indeed if he attempted to do so, his ambition was considered sinful. He could never fully understand this drama; God alone could comprehend it. The function of man's intelligence was "to demonstrate the truth of revealed knowledge, to reconcile diverse and pragmatic experience with the rational pattern of the world as given in faith."[3] Although the medieval period is popularly viewed as the age of faith or belief, it also embraced a large measure of rationalism, because of fundamental desire to substantiate faith through scholarship based on logic and reason. Medieval man certainly had his questions about matters of faith, and this is reflected in his literature and philosophy. His faith was like that of the father of the epileptic child who said to Jesus, "I believe; help my unbelief" (Mark 9:24). Becker considers the thirteenth century to be an age both of reason and of faith:

This is not a paradox. On the contrary, passionate faith and an expert rationalism are apt to be united. Most men (of course I need parentheses here to take care of simple-minded folk and the genuine mystics)—most intelligent men who believe passionately that God's in his heaven and all's right with the world—feel the need of good and sufficient reasons for their faith, all the more so if a few disturbing doubts have crept in to make them uneasy. This is perhaps one of the reasons why the thought of Dante's time was so remorselessly rationalistic. The faith was still intact, surely; but it was just ceasing to be instinctively held—its ablest adherents just becoming conscious that it was held as faith. All the more need, therefore, for proving it up to the hilt. It was precisely because St. Thomas believed in a divinely ordered world that he needed, for his own peace of mind, an impregnable rational proof of a divinely ordered world.[4]

Thus what some critics take to be the simple faith of the Middle Ages was really not simple at all; doubts were weakening the acceptance of religious dogmas and there was a need to sustain belief by use of reason and logic. This mixture of faith and doubt helped to produce a large and important body of rationalistic philosophy and literature which attempted to reconcile faith and reason. One may have profound faith, as Thomas and Dante did, and still have enough doubt to desire rational proof of his beliefs. Faith does not preclude doubt; in effect doubt is probably essential to faith. For in the absence of doubt, doctrine would be accepted as concrete fact, and it would not be necessary to have faith in order to believe it. One need not have faith that there is a sun, since it is seen and experienced in everyday life; pragmatic experience leads one to accept as a fact that the sun exists. Although medieval Christians believed that there was a God, a heaven, and an immortal soul, they also doubted these beliefs. Had they not experienced doubt, they would not have had the need for rational proof of doctrines, and much of the excellent literature and philosophy of the Middle Ages might not exist today. Doubt had stimulated their minds to seek reasons for the mysterious phenomena which confronted them. There was a need to define, to study, and to prove religious dogmas in order to restore the stability that Christianity had enjoyed in the past. To whom were they to turn? Surely there was no better guide than Thomas Aquinas, a man of profound faith who had felt the need to prove rationally his religious convictions. Thomas, in reconciling faith with reason, did for the Christians what Averroës had done for the Arabs and Maimonides for the Jews; all had turned to Aristotle as their master and used logic and empiricism as valid instruments in their philosophy. The *Summa Theologica* fulfilled a basic necessity; it compartmentalized God, the universe, and man in an orderly fashion, appealing to rational thought.

In Spain of the sixteenth century, secularism and insistent questioning of doctrine began to penetrate orthodoxy; this tendency was accelerated by the Reformation. Spain was in dire need of answers to such questions, and she did exactly what the medieval Christian did: she turned to scholastic philosophy, especially that of Thomas Aquinas, to quiet the doubts that plagued her and to protect and sustain her Catholic faith. This revival of Scholasticism was a most important element of the climate of opinion in Golden Age Spain. It had a profound effect on both the religious and the laity, since it was widely taught in the universities and appeared in sermons from the pulpit as well as in the literature of the period.

It may prove difficult at times for twentieth-century man to comprehend the concepts held by medieval Christians and by Spaniards of the Golden Age, since our climate of opinion differs so greatly from theirs. We of the twentieth century have lived through two suicidal wars and countless other devastating events which have caused us to view man as illogical and unreasonable in his behavior. No longer can we readily accept the scholastic idea that human behavior is controlled by reason, nor do we accept the logic which they used to prove their case. The climate of opinion of the twentieth century will not sustain an interest in the philosophical arguments and the methodology utilized in Counter-Reformation Spain. The Spaniard of the sixteenth and seventeenth centuries, like the Christian of the Middle Ages, believed that God, existence, the universe, and man could be studied in a rationalistic way with deductive logic as the methodology. Theology and philosophy, for them the two most important fields of knowledge, helped to reconcile pragmatic experience with revealed truth. The interest in moral philosophy, and particularly in natural-law ethics, in Renaissance and baroque Spain was still quite evident in the eighteenth century, but it is not compatible with the intellectual climate of the nineteenth and twentieth centuries, which are concerned primarily with the union of fact and reason. The study of theology and philosophy has given way in the twentieth century to a preference for history and natural science, a fact readily seen in the curricula of our universities. Twentieth-century man feels the need to study those natural phenomena and recorded events of history which he accepts as concrete facts, rather than the abstract ideas of moral philosophy and religion so dear to the Spaniard of the Golden Age. We of the twentieth century are far removed from the intellectual world of Counter-Reformation Spain, but we should not dismiss as absurd the concepts which were popular at that time. The climate of opinion in

Spain was rational rather than factual, and the Spaniards were very much interested in metaphysics. They preferred the study of theology and philosophy to that of history and science in answering the questions which were important to them.

Spain of the sixteenth and seventeenth centuries found herself in the position of champion of the faith, as she had been during the *reconquista*. Philip II attempted to conserve, fortify, and unify the power and riches which Spain had acquired during the reign of Charles V. Both kings were regarded as protectors of the faith and both had carried their religion beyond their borders with missionary zeal. With equal ardor at home and abroad they fought the sects which had broken from what they held to be orthodox beliefs. The legacy that Charles left his son included not only territory and power but also the costly religious wars and the powerful enemies which were to trouble Spain for many years to come. As a typical leader of his age, Philip seized the opportunity to use his political and religious position to strengthen the Spanish monarchy racially and religiously. The fervor of the *reconquista* was transformed into the zeal of the Counter-Reformation under the reign of Philip. Again the bellicose religious spirit of the Spaniards was brought to bear; they fought the Turks at Lepanto, the Protestants throughout Europe, and the heretics in Spain. This tremendous battle with heresy both abroad and at home was reflected in many facets of Spanish culture, some-times paradoxically, as in the case of the *auto da fe* on the one hand and of the *auto sacramental* on the other. One of the beneficial effects of the Counter-Reformation in Spain was that it produced a moral awakening. The clergy and the laity lacked discipline, customs were ripe for change, and religious nepotism needed to be eliminated. The Council of Trent, in which the Spaniards played an important role, was useful in that it served as a defensive and regenerative religious force protecting and renewing the dogmas, thereby helping to reform the Church.

The intense interest in moral philosophy which characterized the Renaissance and baroque periods increased the popularity of Seneca and caused Stoicism to be Christianized. The Stoics' concept of the law of nature as the principle of moral order and their view of man's relation to the universe attracted Spanish thought at this time. Both Stoicism and skepticism, especially that of Erasmus of Rotterdam, influenced the literature of *desengaño*, which came to be so popular in the seventeenth century. Platonism came into great favor during the Renaissance and had a profound effect on the idealistic philosophy, theology, and literature of the time.[5] Platonic philosophy concerned itself with the moral life; its metaphysics treated the powers of nature, and this encouraged the study of natural philosophy. God was unknowable in essence, but all aspects of nature pointed toward him. In the neoplatonic literature of Spain, the anthropocentric view of man had been propagated by the idealized knights, lovers, and shepherds. Some famous theologians of the time regarded this idealized secular literature as a type of *engaño*, lacking moral discipline and irresponsibly encouraging a form of escapism. In answer to this escapism Spain produced literature which dealt with mysticism, asceticism, and the *desengaño* theme.[6] One of the aims of the Counter-Reformation in Spain, according to Stephen Gilman, was to return to man's existence the final meaning and absolute terms of man's life that were so evident to the medieval mind.

The "undeceived" individual interpreted his perceptions in a different manner after having seen them placed in logical contrast with the infinite and the eternal. He saw a world of confusion, rapidity, and death, but he believed in one regulated and organized by absolute standards, by hierarchy and by category. It was an Aristotelian rather than a Platonic arrangement. As in the *autos* the four elements were restrained from chaotic battle only by divine command. Thus the combination of rigidity and frenzy that characterized the life of Spain as she entered the 17th century.[7]

The intuitive Platonic and Augustinian philosophies faded and were replaced by the pragmatic empiricism of Aristotle and its derivative, Christian Scholasticism.[8] Spain was eclectic, choosing those philosophical systems which best suited her theological position. Diverse schools of thought were popular at different times and in different geographical locations. The University of Alcalá became a center of learning where the philosophical thought of John Duns Scotus was in vogue, while the University of Salamanca was mainly interested in Thomism. With this intellectual activity, Spain produced several well-known thinkers. Francisco de Vitoria was instrumental in introducing Thomas's *Summa Theologica* as a basis for philosophical study at the University of Salamanca. Domingo de Soto was influential in legal studies; Melchor Cano, in critical methodology; Luis de Molina, in ethics; Francisco Suárez, in metaphysics. All of these men were disciples of Thomistic natural-law philosophy, as Bernice Hamilton points out in a chapter devoted to natural law and its implications:

The Thomist version of natural-law theory, which was strongly attacked in all northern universities during the fourteenth and fifteenth centuries and largely jettisoned in Protestant countries, continued unbroken in Spain, and had, indeed, a new flowering during the sixteenth or "golden" century. . . Vitoria and Suárez provide lucid statements of natural-law theory and draw from it some distinctly liberal political conclusions. Domingo de Soto and Molina, each in a different way, contrive to modify these clear statements: Soto by his Augustinian language and his tendency to adopt the jurists', rather than the theologians', definition of natural law; Molina, by his many doubts about the clarity and universal knowability of the natural law, and by his harsher attitude to the old (Moslem) if not to the new (Indian) infidels.[9]

Among these scholars the work of Suárez was particularly important in the revival of Thomistic Scholasticism; his renowned commentary on the *Summa Theologica* was the basis for the study of metaphysics in Spain for many years.

The doctrine of Thomas Aquinas as presented in the *Summa* was the most influential body of thought in the rationalism which held sway in the intellectual climate of Spain during the Counter-Reformation. Of special interest in Thomistic philosophy was natural-law ethics. Thomas Aquinas believed that there was order in the universe under God, who directed all creatures to their ends by a hierarchy of laws: the eternal law—the governance of all things; the natural law—man's participation in the eternal law as a rational being, able to choose between good and evil; the positive law—scriptures which supplement the natural law; and positive human law. Defining law in the general sense as a kind of "rule and measure of acts, whereby man is induced to act or is restrained from action,"[10] Aquinas held that there existed an eternal law by which God directed all creatures to their ends. "Law is nothing else but a dictate of practical reason emanating from the ruler who governs a perfect community. Now it is evident, granted the world is ruled by Divine Providence . . . that the whole community of the universe is governed by Divine Reason. Wherefore the very Idea of the government of things in God the Ruler of the universe, has the nature of a law. And since the Divine Reason's conception of things is not subject to time but is eternal . . . therefore it is that this kind of law must be called eternal."[11] Aquinas believed that God was not indifferent as to whether his plan of creation was carried out, and that thus he ordained that all creatures attain their ends. He believed that God did not direct creatures toward their ends by external force, but rather by intrinsic principles imbedded in their natures. In beings without reason the eternal law was manifest in the physical laws of their natures, whereas in rational creatures it took the form of the natural moral law. Thomas defines natural law as follows:

Since all things subject to Divine providence are ruled and measured by the eternal law . . . it is evident that all things partake somewhat of the eternal law, in so far as, namely, from its being imprinted on them, they derive their respective inclinations to their proper acts and ends. Now among all others, the rational creature is subject to Divine providence in the most excellent way, in so far as it partakes of a share of providence, by being provident both for itself and for others. Wherefore it has a share of the Eternal Reason, whereby it has a natural inclination to its proper act and end: and this participation of the eternal law in the rational creature is called the natural law. . . . the light of natural reason, whereby we discern what is good and what is evil, which is the function of the natural law, is nothing else than an imprint on us of the Divine light. It is therefore evident that the natural law is nothing else than the rational creature's participation of the eternal law.[12]

Aquinas holds that God manifests his plan through natural law, and that man, through natural reason, can know and derive from this law an ethical code. Thomas believed that the natural law was universal and that the first principle "Do good and avoid evil" was self-evident to normal mature human beings as were simple obvious deductions from this principle.

Now as *being* is the first thing that falls under the apprehension simply, so *good* is the first thing that falls under the apprehension of the practical reason, which is directed to action: since every agent acts for an end under the aspect of good. Consequently the first principle in the practical reason is one founded on the notion of good, viz., that *good is that which all things seek after*. Hence this is the first precept of law that *good is to be done and pursued, and evil is to be avoided*. All other precepts of the natural law are based upon this: so that whatever the practical reason naturally apprehends as man's good (or evil) belongs to the precepts of the natural law as something to be done or avoided.[13]

Other general principles based on the first principle were "Do not murder," "Preserve your own being," "Care for your child," and "God must be worshiped." All of these general principles were considered to be easily understood, but the remote conclusions of natural law, derived by a complicated process of reasoning, were difficult to understand.

There belong to the natural law, first, certain most general precepts, that are known to all; and secondly, certain secondary and more detailed precepts, which are, as it were, conclusions following closely from first principles. As to those general principles, the natural law, in the abstract, can nowise be blotted out from men's hearts. But it is blotted out in the case of a particular action, in so far as reason is hindered from applying the general principle to a particular point of practice . . . as to the other, *i.e.*, the secondary precepts, the natural law can be blotted out from the human heart, either by evil persuasions . . . or by vicious customs and corrupt habits.[14]

The more general the principles, the less possible it was for them to be unknown; whereas the more specific they became, the more possibility there was for ignorance and error and for diversity of opinion concerning morality.

Natural law with its self-evident principles presented rules of conduct for man to use as a means to attain his proper end; this was thought to be God's way of guiding man to his ultimate destiny. It was a type of divine light which had been infused into man's mind as an insight into truth. All truth, as Augustine believed, was an illumination and a partial participation in the eternal law. Natural law as a system of ethics did not rely on, nor did it contradict, Christian revelation. In its appeal to man's reason, natural law, which Thomas believed to be universal in nature and existing for all people, was his rational interpretation of Augustine's idea *"credo ut intelligam."* Natural-law philosophy was widespread in its appeal to the authors of Europe[15] and is evident throughout the literature of Golden Age Spain especially in the *comedia* and the *auto sacramental.*

Golden Age drama as an expression of morality falls between the extremes of artistic theory, art for art's sake and utilitarianism. Drama was regarded by the Spanish literary critics of the sixteenth and seventeenth centuries as an instrument with which to imitate reality, the subject and domain of philosophy. The integration of dramatic art and scholastic moral philosophy was an important aspect of the critical theory of this era, which held that drama should both teach and delight. Morality in dramatic form, it was thought, gave pleasure and thus fulfilled both the utilitarian and the aesthetic purposes of art. The playwrights of the Golden Age combined intellectual and emotional elements in a drama which was didactic in that it sought to be persuasive. The new theater which appeared in seventeenth-century Spain produced two groups of dramatic theorists, those who defended and justified this new art form and those who condemned it for not conforming strictly to the precepts of Aristotle. Some of the classicists of the Golden Age held that drama should present an imitation of a known action subject to the discipline of strict form. For these dramatic critics, the proper end of this mimetic endeavor was to direct properly the intellect and emotions. Aristotle believed that imitation was natural to man and a source of delight:

As to its general origin, we may say that Poetry has sprung from two causes, each of them a thing inherent in human nature. The first is the habit of imitation; for to imitate is instinctive with mankind; and man is superior to the other animals, for one thing, in that he is the most imitative of creatures, and learns at first by imitation. Secondly, all men take a natural pleasure in the products of imitation—a pleasure to which the facts of experience bear witness; for even when the original objects are repulsive, as the most objectionable of the lower animals, or dead bodies, we still delight to contemplate their forms as represented in a picture with the utmost fidelity. The explanation of this delight lies in a further characteristic of our species, the appetite for learning; for among human pleasures that of learning is the keenest—not only to the scholarly, but to the rest of mankind as well, no matter how limited their capacity.[16]

Those who followed Aristotle believed that the pleasure derived from this imitation was natural and resulted from man's rational nature and his love for the process of learning.

The use of drama for educational purposes was, of course, nothing new. In ancient Greece poetry was appreciated for its instructive value. Heracleides Ponticus stated that poetry ought to teach (be useful) and give pleasure.[17] This view was later taken by Horace:

Poets aim at giving either profit or delight, or at combining the giving of pleasure with some useful precepts for life. When you are giving precepts of any kind, be succinct, so that receptive minds may easily grasp what you are saying and retain it firmly; when the mind has plenty to cope with, anything superfluous merely goes in one ear and out of the other. Works written to give pleasure should be as true to life as possible, and your play should not demand belief for just anything that catches your fancy; you should not let the ogress Lamia gobble up a child, and later bring it out of her belly alive. The centuries of the elder citizens will disapprove of works lacking in edification, while the haughty Ramnes will have nothing to do with plays that are too serious.[18]

While Horace held that the ends of art were either to delight *or* to instruct, Spanish as well as other European critics interpreted these views to mean that art ought to teach *and* delight (*enseñar deleitando*). In William McCrary's study of Horace's theories and their relation to the *comedia* he states: "Juan de la Cueva . . . not only advocates the Horatian formula but regards any deviation from its time honored ends as tantamount to a literary transgression:

> Si en esas obras que te vas cansando
> ni enseñas, ni deleitas, que es oficio
> de los que siguen los que vas mostrando:
> luego, razón será imputarle a vicio
> al que de esto se aparta en su poesía.

Alonso López becomes more specific in his statement of the traditional formula:

Tres prouechos traen estas artes . . . el uno es
alterar y quietar las passiones del alma a
sus tiempos convenientes, el segundo mejorar
las costumbres, el tercero . . . el entretenimiento.

To Cascales, the idea of imitation is distinctly an instrumental concept:

El fin de la poesía es agradar y aprovechar
imitando: de modo que el Poema no basta ser
agradable, sino provechoso y moral: como
quien es imitación de la vida, espejo
de las costumbres, imagen de la verdad.

Poetry's purposes, therefore, are achieved by imitation. The result of such mimesis renders reality a mirror of life, or an image of truth, which satisfies both the aesthetic and the moral objects of art."[19]

After discussing the form and the purpose of dramatic art, the Spanish theorists invariably went on to consider the moral rather than the aesthetic aspects of that art. While the structure of Golden Age drama reflects Aristotelian influence, the moral preoccupation of the playwrights derived from Horace and Seneca. Moral doctrine was a proper object of drama, because it satisfied both the utilitarian and the aesthetic ends of art in that its dramatic treatment was, as Aristotle implied, a pleasurable imitation.

That natural-law theory played a vital role in the integration of moral doctrine and art in the Golden Age can readily be seen in the drama where it is most coherently expressed, particularly in the *auto sacramentales* of Calderón de la Barca. Natural law is so fundamental to some dramas, both religious and secular, that without an understanding of the tenets of this philosophical system the ideological themes which form the very core of the works may elude the reader.

While a catalog or index of references to natural law in the broader spectrum of Golden Age theater might have its uses, the importance of the relationship of this ethical system to the drama can best be demonstrated by textual analysis of representative plays in which natural law is essential to the main themes. Such an examination not only facilitates a fuller appreciation of these dramas, but also by giving the reader a broader knowledge of the intellectual climate of the period enables him to gain a better understanding of other contemporaneous works. In addition to the literary analyses of specific works, this study will include a chapter on the *auto sacramental* as a genre in the hope of facilitating the comprehension of these frequently misunderstood dramatic pieces. Close textual explication of Lope de Vega's *Fuenteovejuna*, Tirso de Molina's *La mejor espigadera*, and three of Calderón de la Barca's *autos, El gran teatro del mundo, No hay más fortuna que Dios,* and *A Dios por razón de estado* indicates the degree to which these authors used the idea of natural law and illustrates the necessity of understanding this philosophical doctrine and the intellectual climate in which it flourished as a prerequisite to the appreciation of the drama of Golden Age Spain.

Chapter Two

Fuenteovejuna

In the dramatic work of Lope de Vega natural law appears most coherently in the central ideological theme of one of his more complex plays, *Fuenteovejuna*.[1] This play treats an event of moral and metaphysical significance which Lope has extracted from the Rades Andrada's *Chronicle*.[2] There is a mutual interdependence of the historic and metaphysical implications which may be studied as an ethical problem.[3] The central ideological theme of justice in *Fuenteovejuna* can be analyzed to demonstrate that the dramatic action on all levels and the ultimate meaning follow the order of natural law according to Aristotelian-Thomistic ethics. Lope dramatizes a historical fact with metaphysical significance—"the triumph of order over chaos."[4] The ultimate violence which is found in the rebellion of the villagers and in the murder of the Comendador is justified according to natural law, and results in an atmosphere of order and harmony. In order to comprehend the theme of poetic justice which the action demonstrates,[5] one must trace back to their first cause the events which constitute the climax of the play. In *Fuenteovejuna* the Comendador is the first cause; he is not merely an external instrument of the *peripetia*, but rather is tied in with the action as a whole, as the agent who initiates the chain of causality which in the end turns back on him in the form of punishment. His immoral acts produce the catastrophe and ultimately his own death.

In the sixteenth and seventeenth centuries the law of punishment was believed to be based on the law of nature and affirmation of experience, but was always ascribed to God.[6] In *Fuenteovejuna* the punishment demonstrates two aspects of the theme: historical calamities are shown to be punishments of sin permitted by God, and tyrants are assured that God is not helpless before their temporal power, but that he will ultimately destroy them after having used them. The law of punishment has as its basis the natural law, attributed to God, from which are derived obligation and sanction. Following the tenets of natural law, moral obligation cannot come from one's fellow man, for as moral beings all men are equal; nor can it come from oneself, since a lawmaker can repeal his own law. Natural law states that moral obligation comes from God, who determines through eternal law the relationship between the observance of moral law and man's destiny, making the attainment of man's proper end the province of God. The Creator's will and intellect are made manifest to man through natural law, the primary source of obligation; from it alone civil laws derive their binding force.

The concept of obligation leads to that of sanction, which the dramatist expresses in the form of poetic justice. The sense of obligation resulting from a final cause urges man to act but does not destroy his free will, and so provides a motive strong enough to attract man to free acts of obedience.[7] The function of sanction is to induce man to keep the law and dissuade him from breaking it, and to restore the order of justice after the law has been broken. A natural sanction may follow from the nature of the act performed, as nausea may follow intemperance. A positive sanction is determined by the lawgiver and has no natural connection with a given act.

The natural law cannot have positive sanctions, for any direct revelation of God's will would be divine positive law. Observance of the natural law brings about harmony between man's acts and his nature. But in actual experience this harmony is not always realized; sanction is not perfect here on earth. Aquinas holds that God is not indifferent as to whether his law is obeyed or not, and therefore he provides a perfect sanction to the natural law after this life. This perfect sanction is the gain or loss of man's salvation; no stronger sanction may be applied without privation of man's free will.

Natural law imposes obligations on man to make his actions conform to the norm of morality as a means to the achievement of his proper destiny. Natural law, in decreeing such obligations for man, also gives him the right to fulfill them and the right to prevent others from interfering with their realization. Thus, there are rights which come from natural law. God, the Author of natural law and natural God-given rights, wills the end and also wills the means necessary to the end.

"St. Thomas Aquinas had thought of God as the General of an Army, governing men toward a final end, which is His victory. Renaissance humanists prefer the metaphor of the Dramatist, which honors God by removing Him from the scene of conflict to the throne of a Poet's glory."[8] The theological use of drama in the Golden Age is one of moral warning by means of skillfully composed works in which the artist first imitates, then idealizes nature and reality, bringing into the drama everything which is pertinent in order to present the totality and integrity of nature in a given case. We find in these plays the revelation of divine purpose and plan. God, the ultimate Dramatist, presides over the universe, in which individual souls play their assigned roles.

This divine purpose and plan of nature is presented by Lope in the four action-levels of *Fuenteovejuna*. Although plots in Golden Age drama are often complicated, the incidents in these plots steadily merge with each other until finally at the end of the play, and only at the end, one sees that the seemingly disjointed facets of the subplots give more significance to the major theme, and make a more meaningful unity.[9] As Professor William C. McCrary has observed, "Lope has established four separate, but not independent actions, which communicate the significance of the moment through as many levels of corresponding implications, a procedure which adds to the purely histrionic the dimensions of the epic. The first of these involves the love duet of Laurencia and Frondoso; the second concerns the collective reality of the village itself of which the lovers are citizens; the third is centered on Ciudad Real; and the fourth engages the entire Iberian Peninsula."[10] In this manner the four independent action-levels of *Fuenteovejuna* merge into the one central theme of justice. The pattern of movement of the play is complex but orderly. This order stems from and conforms to the natural law according to Aristotelian-Thomistic principles.[11] From the very beginning of the play the harmony of the natural order has been disrupted on every level by the Comendador's morally reprehensible behavior. Scenes 1 and 2 of Act 1 deal with disorder on both the national and regional levels. The Comendador, by seducing the young Maestre into helping him in his plan of treason at Ciudad Real, has threatened the unity of the whole kingdom. He has no moral right to foment sedition against the monarchy, which has the right to a peaceful and orderly existence.

Wherefore it is evident that the unity to which sedition is opposed is the unity of law and common good: whence it follows manifestly that sedition is opposed to justice and the common good. . . .

Accordingly the sin of sedition is first and chiefly in its authors, who sin most grievously; and secondly it is in those who are led by them to disturb the common good.[12]

By his disruption of the peaceful and orderly existence of the monarchy, the Comendador has opposed the common good of the kingdom. He has become habitually tyrannical, working for his own selfish aims and harming the people of Fuenteovejuna.

Scenes 3 and 4 of Act 1 are concerned with the village of Fuenteovejuna and with Laurencia and Frondoso. Here the order is disrupted on the village level and in the relationship of Laurencia and Frondoso. Because of the Comendador's forced attentions, Laurencia's behavior has been altered; she wants nothing to do with love or men. The only thing she is able to love at this point is her *propio honor;* and as a noble, the Comendador has no honorable intentions toward a peasant girl, since marriage between them is unacceptable. Frondoso rescues Laurencia from the immoral advances of the Comendador, and while as a peasant he may not have the legal right to do so (Act 1, scene 12), he has the moral right and duty to act as he does according to natural law. One may come to the assistance of another whose life, or goods equivalent to life, are unjustly attacked. Chastity is considered by natural law to be a good which is equivalent to life.

The four action-levels are tied together by the themes of sedition and rape on the part of the Comendador,[13] and by the love of Laurencia and Frondoso, which is representative of the cohesive element of mankind, harmony. In scene 5 we know that the rupture of order on the national and regional levels has definitely taken place; the Maestre has taken Ciudad Real. The disruption of order on all levels becomes complete in Act 2, and the tension builds. The Comendador forcibly carries off Jacinta to be a camp follower for the army, thus usurping her basic rights. Mengo attempts to save Jacinta by appealing to the Comendador, but, instead of heeding the villager's plea, the tyrant has him punished:

MENGO.   Señor, si piedad os mueve
              de suceso tan injusto,
              castigad estos soldados,
              que con vuestro nombre agora
              roban una labradora
              a esposo y padres honrados;
              y dadme licencia a mí
              que se la pueda llevar.
COMENDADOR.   Licencia les quiero dar . . .
              para vengarse de ti.
              Suelta la honda.[14]

The Comendador appears at Frondoso and Laurencia's wedding feast and carries off both the bride and the bridegroom. As a final insult to the whole village, he takes the staff of authority from the *alcalde*, Esteban, and breaks it over the elder's head. Thus in the first two acts, harmony has been disrupted from its lowest and most basic level, that of individual love, to its highest level—the monarchy. These four levels will interweave until the end of the play, when they will fuse into one action of violence which will result in the restoration of harmony and unity to the whole of Spain. As the chain of causality progresses on all levels, the tension grows until it explodes in the form of a revolt. The play does not end, however, with an outburst of violence; for this would be merely an exposition of a historical event.[15] Rather, Lope ends it with a definite moral lesson; justice, restoring harmony, triumphs on all levels.

The theme of restoration of order begins in Act 3 and gradually becomes dominant. In the first scene the village elders meet to discuss what they must do. The Maestre has been defeated in battle by the king and order has been restored everywhere in the peninsula, but nothing will be corrected until justice has triumphed in this last outpost, Fuenteovejuna. Something must be done to bring harmony to the village; the outrageous behavior of the Comendador can no longer be tolerated:

REGIDOR.   Ya todo el árbol de paciencia roto
              corre la nave de temor perdida.
              La hija quitan con tan gran fiereza
              a un hombre honrado, de quien es regida

<table>
<tr><td></td><td>la patria en que vivís, y en la cabeza
la vara quiebran tan injustamente.
¿Qué esclavo se trató con más bajeza?</td></tr>
<tr><td>JUAN ROJO.</td><td>¿Qué es lo que quieres tú que el pueblo intente?</td></tr>
<tr><td>REGIDOR.</td><td>Morir, o dar la muerte a los tiranos,
pues somos muchos, y ellos poca gente.</td></tr>
</table>

(845)

The climax is reached in scene 3 of the final act as Laurencia comes onto the stage in a disheveled state and incites the villagers to revolt. The Comendador is about to hang Frondoso without a trial—the ultimate attempted injustice which justifies the violence that will take place:

LAURENCIA.	¿Vosotros sois hombres nobles?
	¿Vosotros padres y deudos?
	¿Vosotros, que no se os rompen
	las entrañas de dolor,
	de verme en tantos dolores?
	Ovejas sois, bien lo dice
	de Fuenteovejuna el nombre
	Dadme unas armas a mí,
	pues sois piedras, pues sois bronces,
	. . . .
	A Frondoso quiere ya,
	sin sentencia, sin pregones,
	colgar el Comendador
	de una almena de la torre;
	de todos hará lo mismo;
	y yo me huelgo, medio-hombres,
	porque quede sin mujeres
	esta villa honrada, y torne
	aquel siglo de amazonas,
	eterno espanto del orbe.

(846)

Natural law decrees that man has a right not only to life itself, but to a life fit for a rational being. The right includes the possession of certain goods that are virtually equivalent to life itself. Natural law permits the use of force, even the killing of an unjust aggressor (in this case the Comendador) to defend such goods. The goods which are considered to be almost equivalent to life are limbs and faculties, liberty, chastity, and material goods of great value.[16] Since the Comendador's acts of violence against the nation, the region, the village, and the individuals, deny both the right to life and the right to goods equivalent to life, they cannot be allowed to continue unrestrained. As a last resort, violence is justified to end these outrages.

Natural law holds that government has a right to exist and a right to put down rebellion using means that are not intrinsically evil.[17] The misuse of power in itself does not take away the right to that power. Since those who govern are fallible human beings, minor abuses of power are apt to occur frequently and serious ones from time to time. Such abuses do not justify rebellion against the state, although they do call for protest. Against petty unjust acts of a ruler, natural law permits passive resistance and even active resistance short of force. Tyrants, however, usually deny the opportunity of peaceful means of dissent. In this case the Comendador does not pay heed to the pleas and petitions of the villagers. When admonished politely by Esteban for speaking too freely, the Comendador answers sarcastically,

> ¡Oh, qué villano elocuente!
> ¡Ah Flores!, haz que le den
> la *Política*, en que lea,
> de Aristóteles.[18]
>
> (837)

Under natural law forceful resistance is permitted against a tyrant who does not pay heed to peaceful petitions and is attempting to inflict serious personal harm. In this case the ruler becomes an unjust aggressor, and self-defense may be employed against him. Although forceful resistance might appear to be inexpedient, it is not against natural law if the rules of blameless self-defense are followed. The people of Fuenteovejuna have the right to life and its equivalents, and to the means to preserve these against the unjust aggressions of the Comendador. Thus the organized, armed resistance of the village to a constituted authority, the Comendador, is a rebellion which is justified according to natural law. The violence that they commit is an act of blameless self-defense. The repelling of force with force, ordinarily handled by the civil government, must at times be done by individuals. It is in accordance with natural law to repel force with force if all other defenses have been exhausted, and if the motive of this force is self-defense. Forceful resistance may be used at the time of attack but no more injury than necessary may be inflicted. In granting the right to life, natural law gives man the right to protect that life by any means that is not intrinsically wrong.

The Comendador has acted in such a way as to forfeit the office which was given to him. He has shown no respect for human rights on the level either of the peasant or of the king. His has certainly been a constant and excessive tyranny; because of this, the rebellion is justified. The government has been habitually tyrannical and has lost sight of the common good. The Comendador has used the government to promote his own ends. The oppressed people see no prospect of a change within a reasonable time. All legal and peaceful means to recall the Comendador to a sense of duty have been exhausted. He shows no respect for the basic laws of the village or for the monarchy. There is a reasonable probability that the rebellion will be successful. The judgment that the Comendador's rule is tyrannical is accepted by a large and well-distributed number of citizens (*viejo, muchacho, mujer, hombre, rollizo, desnudo*, and *gordo*),[19] indicating that it is representative of the people as a whole. The natural law condemns tyranny in government as one of the worst crimes because it works its injustice on many people.

A tyrannical government is not just, because it is directed, not to the common good, but to the private good of the ruler, as the Philosopher states (*Polit*. iii. 5; *Ethic*. viii. 10). Consequently there is no sedition in disturbing a government of this kind, unless indeed the tyrant's rule be disturbed so inordinately, that his subjects suffer greater harm from the consequent disturbance than from the tyrant's government. Indeed it is the tyrant rather that is guilty of sedition, since he encourages discord and sedition among his subjects, that he may lord over them more securely; for this is tyranny, being conducive to the private good of the ruler, and to the injury of the multitude.[20]

The rebellion of Fuenteovejuna is a symbol of retributive justice and national self-defense against the atrocities and barbarities of an unjust ruler. Retributive justice has been applied by the people;[21] distributive justice—the fair and proper distribution of public benefits and burdens—is accomplished by the king, who pardons the repentant young Maestre and forgives the people of Fuenteovejuna. By assuming governance of the village until a new *comendador* can be found, the king takes the last step toward the restoration of order in the monarchy. The collective crimes of the Comendador have been punished, the village of Fuenteovejuna has been restored to order, and harmony now reigns on all levels.

The central ideological theme in *Fuenteovejuna*, dramatized on four levels, is the development of the principle of poetic justice which results in the achievement of harmony. Following the order of the natural law, Lope de Vega has idealized the metaphysical significance of the triumph of order over chaos through the medium of the villagers, who justly resort to revolution and murder to secure the return of harmony in Fuenteovejuna.

Chapter Three

La mejor espigadera

While natural-law philosophy appears less frequently in Tirso de Molina's dramas than in those of Lope de Vega and Calderón de la Barca, it is sometimes present in juxtaposition with the main theme of the plays. In *La mejor espigadera*, Tirso dramatizes an ethical problem related to those of his day by bringing biblical characters and customs to a contemporary audience, that of Counter-Reformation Spain. A well-trained biblical scholar like most Golden Age dramatists, Tirso de Molina followed the popular tradition of bringing the message of the Bible to the secular audience of his era in an entertaining and dignified manner. His purpose was twofold: to teach and to amuse his public, thereby using the medium of drama for didactic purposes, a common practice, as we have seen, in Golden Age Spain. Consequently the lessons of morality in his Old Testament plays are communicated by the dramatic interplay of vice and virtue.[1] Carefully utilizing the biblical narratives and skillfully harmonizing dramatic, comic, and lyric elements to exemplify virtue and to condemn vice, he directs a homily to his audience. Without including in these plays any article of faith contrary to Catholicism, he adds to the biblical narrative as he sees fit, not only to sermonize effectively but also to make the story more palatable to his public.[2]

In *La mejor espigadera* Tirso at times incorporates the actual words of the Bible into the text of his play but avoids a literal representation of the biblical account.[3] The Book of Ruth is laconic in its description of the heroine's life and mission; the author repeats a well-known story with the purpose of drawing attention both to Ruth's loyalty to Naomi and to Israel's messianic hope (Ruth 4:17, 18–22). He underlines the Moabite background of Ruth and emphasizes the divine intention that is fulfilled at the climax of the story (4: 13–18). Ruth, a native of a country hostile to Israel, obtains an honorable position among the people of Judah and becomes an

ancestor of the illustrious king David. Going beyond the simple
biblical narrative and utilizing the conventional formulae of the
comedia, Tirso dramatizes the rightness and wrongness of his
characters' actions, presenting an ethical problem that is related to
natural law—man's obligation to his fellow man in society. Up to the
first part of Act 3 Tirso illustrates the communal spirit of man in
society through Naomi, Ruth, and Boaz. In opposition to their
charitable behavior he condemns the avarice of Elimelech and his
sons. The biblical story of Ruth is not brought to the stage until the
third act, and then it is embellished with certain additions.

Through his additions to the biblical text, Tirso has created well-
defined characters who represent in varying degrees man's obligation
to love his fellow man and to aid him in attaining his final end, a
basic tenet of natural law. Parallel to the main theme of charity are
the motifs of divine providence and just government which add
theological and philosophical dimensions to the play by alluding to
the fact that God is involved in the material and spiritual affairs of
man, leading him to his final destiny.[4] Naomi, Ruth, and Boaz as
exemplary figures help their fellow man by their charitable deeds,
while Elimelech and his sons ignore their social responsibilities
because of their intemperate interest in material goods.

In the first act Tirso provides a magnificent example of baroque
antithesis in the two characters Elimelech and Naomi, the one representing vice and the other virtue. Tirso introduces the sin of avarice
in the character of Elimelech, who stands at the center of the ethical
problem as a man who disobeys God's law by being irresponsible to
his fellow man. According to natural law, a man in a responsible
position such as Elimelech's has the duty to look after the well-being
of his fellow men. The concepts of charity, just government, and
eternal law are introduced as the peasants speak of Elimelech:

> HERBEL. ¡Qué mal que le cuadra el nombre
> de Elimelec!
> ASER. Significa
> Dios mío, porque os asombre.
> GOMOR. Mal el ser Dios se le aplica
> a tan avariento hombre,
> que Dios a todos mantiene,
> y más guardando su ley.

HERBEL.   *Rey* a interpretarse viene
              Elimelec.
LISIS.   ¡Qué mal rey
              quien guardando el trigo tiene
              y a ningún pobre recibe!
ASER.   Es alma el rey, que del modo
              que vida al cuerpo apercibe,
              y estando toda en el todo,
              toda en cualquier parte vive;
              así el rey tiene de estar
              dando a todo el reino ser,
              y en cualquier parte o lugar
              todo lo ha de socorrer
              y sus miembros sustentar.
                            (982)

Tirso includes three levels of the natural and eternal laws by having the peasants, through natural reason, present the argument that the landowner is responsible for his workers in the same way that a king is for his subjects and God for his creatures. Disobeying natural law, Elimelech chooses not to conform to the norm of morality, going against human nature and ignoring his responsibilities to his workers. The norm of morality, a standard to which men compare human acts to determine their goodness or badness, is not treated expressly by Aquinas; he includes it, however, in his discussion of the eternal and natural laws:

Due order to an end is measured by some rule. In things that act according to nature, this rule is the natural force that inclines them to that end. When therefore an action proceeds from a natural force, in accord with the natural inclination to an end, then the action is said to be right. . .
    Now in those things that are done by the will, the proximate rule is the human reason, while the supreme rule is the Eternal Law. When, therefore, a human action tends to the end, according to the order of reason and of the Eternal Law, then that action is right: but when it turns aside from that rectitude, then it is said to be a sin. Now it is evident from what has been said (Q. 19, AA. 3,4) that every voluntary action that turns aside from the order of reason and of the Eternal Law, is evil, and that every good action is in accord

with reason and the Eternal Law. Hence it follows that a human action is right or sinful by reason of its being good or evil.[5]

In *La mejor espigadera* the norm of morality is sufficiently well known to be self-evident even to the peasants, hence Elimelech has no excuse for not adhering to it. There is no doubt that his behavior is contrary to this norm. His acts, unworthy of a rational creature, do not lead to the morally correct end; indeed they are contrary to human nature and cause disharmony among those who surround him.

Natural law proclaims that man is not a solitary being, but a part of God's creation, and as such he must fit himself into the total scheme of this creation and occupy the place to which his individual nature suits him. Viewing human nature in all of its aspects, natural law considers man a created being in his relation to God, a social being in his relation to his fellow man, and a possessive being in his relation to the goods of the earth. In its relation to that which is above man, human nature is created by and contingent on God; through natural reason man is able to comprehend his duties to God of obedience and worship. On man's own level, human nature is considered to be social; man adheres to a family unit and is made for companionship with his fellow man, on whom he depends to supply his needs and develop his abilities. Human nature in its relation to things beneath man is taken to be possessive; man needs the use of material things for the maintenance of life itself. Thus there are three essential aspects of human nature: man is a created, a social, and a possessive being. Following natural-law ethics, the norm of morality must take into consideration all three aspects. Elimelech, captive of his vice, recognizes only the possessive part of his nature, while the peasants, following natural reason, point out his complete disregard for the other two elements.

Elimelech's behavior is out of harmony with the demands of all three essential relations of human nature and creates physical and metaphysical disharmony. He ignores man's dependence on God. Instead of promoting a social life which functions well and concurs with natural law, he disrupts the harmony of human society with complete disregard for his fellow man. In disobedience to natural law, he relies solely on the use of material things in his quest for happiness, stressing too much the possessive aspect of human nature.[6]

Greed has blinded Elimelech to his dependent relationship to God and to his social responsibilities. Assuming that man has complete dominion over possessions, Elimelech goes against God's intentions when he does not use his wealth to aid his fellow man in attaining his ultimate end. He attempts to escape the responsibilities of society by taking his material goods to Moab.

> No he de estar más en Belén,
> no ha de verme más Judá
> adonde enfado me den
> holgazanes de Efratá.
> Todo el ganado prevén,
>   (*A su hijo.*)
> bestias, caballos, camellos;
> mi hacienda en los carros carga,
> que a Moab he de ir con ellos,
> pues no es la jornada larga
> ni hallaré pobres entre ellos.
>   (988)

Elimelech carries his desire of assuring his own safety and prosperity to an extreme by gathering up his material goods and leaving the area of the famine. It is God's intention, according to natural law, that man have dominion over material things, but always under God's greater dominion. Elimelech fails to recognize that God directs all things to their ends by the nature he gives them, and that man's complete human nature as manifested to him through natural reason is the proximate norm of morality which he must follow. In his pursuit of happiness Elimelech has placed too much emphasis on goods of fortune, thinking that these make men happy. Finite external things with which man can surround himself in the present life, such as wealth, honor, fame, position, power, and influence, are meant to be means, not ends in themselves. Elimelech has gone counter to natural law in using worldly goods as ends rather than as means. Although Elimelech might not be considered the primary personage in the play as a whole his character is germane to the theme of charity and central to the ethical problem, man's social obligation to his fellow man, which the drama so aptly presents.

On the positive side the theme of charity is developed through the characters of Naomi, Boaz, and especially Ruth; their ideal behavior is a strong contrast to Elimelech's avarice. Naomi, as a moral being, is Elimelech's opposite; she is a virtuous woman who acknowledges the existence of a supreme being and lives according to natural law. In helping the peasants, she realizes that the material goods which she owns come from God, and should be used to relieve the hunger that the peasants are suffering. Disobeying Elimelech and following her conscience, she gives alms to the poor.

> No está en casa mi marido;
> ojalá pobres vinieran,
> ques pues Dios me ha enriquecido,
> con abundancia comieran
> lo que les he prevenido.[7]
>
> (983)

The cruelty of the famine and Elimelech's lack of social responsibility culminate in the scene in which Zefara and Jaleel, a starving husband and wife, debate whether it is licit to eat their own child. It is self-evident that eating one's child is contrary to natural law and human nature. Elimelech's lack of charity has led to this pitiful situation, which Naomi alleviates by giving them some bread and lamb.

Naomi's convictions coincide with those of the elders, who recognize Elimelech's social and moral responsibilities, and she requests that he give some of his material wealth to the poor. Elimelech, who lacks respect for the poor, calling them *viles heces, basura, hormigas viles, infames, harpías monstruosas, moscas enfadosas, inútiles y asquerosas, reliquias bajas, polillas crueles, huéspedes infames,* is infuriated by this request.

> ¿Los jueces mi pan a mí
> para dar a pobres? ¡Bueno!
> ¿Lo que yo sembré y cogí?
> ¿Yo mi trigo, mi centeno
> a pobres? Ponzoña sí.
> Muera la gente villana
> de hambre, que yo no doy
> a quien, con vida holgazana,
> se come su hacienda hoy
> sin reparar que hay mañana.

Antes pegaré a mis trojes
fuego, y vaciaré mi vino.
(985-86)

Elimelech not only refuses to help the peasants himself, but angrily
chides Naomi for giving them alms. This prompts Zefara to curse the
landlord:

Permita Dios que no goces
tus avarientos regalos;
púdranse tus viles mieses,
vinagre el vino se torne
los lobos coman tus reses,
jamás tus techos adorne
el otoño en sus tres meses.
De tu hacienda despojado
patrias extrañas mendigues;
no halles hospicio en poblado,
y como al pobre persigues
del rico seas mal tratado.
Fáltete el Dios en que esperas,
y ejecute sus castigos
en esas entrañas fieras;
entre tus más enemigos
fuera de tu patria mueras.
No vuelvas más a Belén,
ni tus trabajos amansen,
ni sepultura te den
en que tus güesos descansen
con los de tu padre . . .
(986)

These prophetic curses will be fulfilled; Tirso here brings in the theme
of divine providence by implying that it is God's will that Elimelech be
punished. Naomi, speaking to her sons, warns them not to follow their
father's example, and advises them to adhere to the norm of morality
and right reason.

De Dios, hijos, el mendigo
es pupilo y menor es;
y el rico, tutor y abrigo

de los pequeños y hambrientos.
Si menores nuestros son,
dejad viles pensamientos,
que no es conforme a razón
negarles sus alimentos.
                                    (987)

By use of right reason as it applies to human nature in all its parts and relations, Naomi deduces the morally good acts which man ought to perform. She expresses the proximate norm of morality which is related to human nature and is immediately applicable to her sons' acts, and she informs them of the ultimate norm of morality, related to the divine nature, by advising them that human activity ought to resemble divine activity. Although Naomi is not the central personage in this play, she is an important element in the plot, exemplifying a morally good woman who conforms to right reason, the norm of morality, and tradition in following her conscience and aiding the poor.

Tirso has chosen a pagan, Ruth, who is provident for her fellow man in a special way, to be the central figure illustrating the theme of charity.[8] From the beginning of the dramatic action Ruth realizes that she has been chosen by God to fulfill a special role in life.

La ley aborrezco incierta
de mi ciega idolatría.
al Dios de Israel me inclino
de un oráculo divino
que estimo por profecía.
Sé que un esposo me espera,
el más noble de Efratá,
que en mí sucesión tendrá
dilatado de manera
que llegue su última rama
al cielo más eminente,
para que en su flor se asiente
un Rey-Dios que a Israel ama.
                                    (992)

Tirso introduces this oracle to emphasize the providential role of Ruth, whose actions follow the principles of natural law and thereby

fulfill the mandates of God's plan of creation, the eternal law.[9] The
supernatural element appears again in the prophecy pronounced by
Ruth's servant in Act 2:

> . . . que el Cielo
> (si no es que amor desatine),
> en historias y en estatuas
> quiere que te inmortalices.
>
> . . . .
>
> el sueño alegre predice
> la casa real de Bohoz;
> y que la piedra sublime
> de quien nacerá la vara
> que el más alto Cielo humille,
> será una mujer gentil
> de Moab, bella y humilde,
> que casándose con él,
> el cordero amante obligue,
> que de los pastos sabrosos,
> donde *ab aeterno* reside,
> al monte de Judá baje
> para que a Dagón derribe.
> Por una idólatra, en fin,
> y un príncipe de la estirpe
> de Bohoz ha de gozar
> el mundo al que el Cielo rige,
> y llamándose el Mesías
> hará hazañas que conquisten
> desde la cuna del sol
> hasta su túmulo triste.
>
> (1007)

Because of this oracle Ruth is convinced and later convinces her
father that she must give up her position as princess of Moab and
marry Mahlon. This is preordained, as she explains: "Mi ventura el
Cielo ordena" (1010). Ruth, in adhering to the eternal law, freely
guides herself to her end, and freely cooperates with God in achieving
the purpose of her creation. According to Thomas, God has created
causes which of their very essence are free and contingent. He believes
that since nothing resists the divine will, it follows not only that
those things happen that God wills to happen, but that they happen

necessarily or contingently according to his will. The will of God does not determine the nature of a free act, but only the fact of its existence; Thomas insists that predestination does not preclude free will.[10] Thus Ruth, acting in accordance with the eternal law, freely chooses to perform charitable deeds.

In the first two acts Tirso has established the themes and the ethical problem and has created well-motivated characters, preparing his audience for the unexpected denouement. In Act 3 the playwright necessarily focuses on the biblical narrative, amplifying and interpreting it in accordance with the demands of poetic justice in order to enhance the themes of providence and charity. Elimelech and his two sons have been killed, leaving Naomi without a family in a foreign land. Naomi accepts the disasters that have befallen her family as the will of God. Telling her son Mahlon of Elimelech's death she says:

> El oro, joyas y galas
> en que la avaricia tiene
> cifrada su frágil dicha,
> ya son males, que no bienes;
> castigo del Cielo justo,
> con que a los pobres pretende
> vengar de nuestra crueldad
> que es Dios padre de inocentes.
> Negásteisles el sustento
> siendo deudos o parientes.
> (994)

Speaking to her daughters-in-law of the deaths of Mahlon and Chilion, Naomi acknowledges the punishment of God:

> Hijas, ya que Dios me ha dado
> el castigo merecido,
>
> . . . .
> ... con miserable castigo
> quisieron vengar los Cielos
> en mis hijos el dejar
> su Dios y ley verdadera;
> de la ambición lisonjera
> se dejaron engañar.

De dios la justicia estimo,
como su esclava le adoro.
(1013)

Her sons not only gave up their religion, which is considered in the play to be the true faith, but also misused their material goods. They were irrational opportunists who lived haphazardly without thinking of their ultimate destiny.[11] After the death of her husband, Ruth decides to go with her mother-in-law to Bethlehem, believing that her going has been preordained:

> Madre, no es justo que ansí
> a quien te adora despidas.
> Un alma vive en tres vidas;
> quien las da ser es Nohemí.
> Yo no te pienso dejar,
> que esto mi ventura ordena.
> (1013)

Although Ruth is inclined to follow the law of God, it is of her own free will that she decides not to leave Naomi. Tirso brings in the theme of maintaining the true faith, a popular topic in Spain of the Counter-Reformation, by showing how Mahlon and Chilion have sinned in going against their faith, and how Ruth, following the will of God, is converted to Judaism.

In Act 3 Tirso adds details to the drama that are not found in the Bible, making the outcome of the play more logical and at the same time increasing the pathos of the widow's situation. The dramatic character Ruth is fully developed in this act in which as a virtuous widow she chooses to glean in order to support Naomi, and later marries the wealthy landowner Boaz. When Naomi and Ruth arrive in Bethlehem they seek alms from relatives, but are refused in spite of the fact that Bethlehem is enjoying a good crop. On the basis of the good harvest, Ruth decides to go to Boaz's fields in order to gather leftover grain. The Bible says nothing of the good crop nor does it mention that Ruth and Naomi asked their relatives for alms. In giving up her title as princess of Moab and taking on the humble status of gleaner, Ruth has given more credence to spiritual than to material goods. By caring for Naomi she excels in virtue, proving to be an

especially prudent woman.[12] Her goodness is widely recognized by
those who work with her and know her. Boaz, a virtuous man
himself,[13] praises Ruth's sense of *caritas* as he says to her:

> Ya sé que el reino dejas
> a tu virtud debido,
> la patria en que naciste,
> el tálamo ofrecido,
> la ley que cuerda truecas,
> por la que el dedo ha escrito
> de Dios, que dió a Moisés,
> nuestro primer caudillo.
> La caridad más nueva
> que vieron nuestros siglos
> que con tu suegra usaste,
> pues al humildo oficio
> de espigadera pobre
> el trono has reducido
> por sólo sustentalla
> del majestuoso sitio.
>
> (1021)

In contrast to Elimelech's avarice and disregard for the law of God,
Ruth's actions are prudent because they are charitable. The three
virtuous characters, Ruth, Boaz, and Naomi, who have acted according to right reason and have been charitable to their fellow man, are
bound together by the preordained marriage of Ruth and Boaz. Tirso
again brings in the supernatural element by having Ruth and Boaz
receive an inclination to marry through oracles and visions. When
Ruth lies at the feet of Boaz in the fields she acknowledges celestial
influence in her behavior toward him:

> Persuasiones de Nohemí;
> celestiales influencias
> que en proféticos avisos
> certifican sus promesas,
> me traen . . .
>
> (1025)

In speaking of his future marriage Boaz tells of a vision which he
believes comes from God:

En un misterioso sueño
quiso el Cielo revelarme
que no tengo de casarme,
ni mi amor llamará dueño
sino a una mujer moabita,
cuya virtud y humildad
honre mi posteridad
con descendencia infinita.
(1018)

Boaz, in choosing to marry Ruth, fulfills his preordained role; he knows that from his lineage will come the Messiah:

Si en una mujer gentil
he de tener descendencia
de quien proceda el Mesías
que Israel tanto ha que aspera,
sea Rut, piadoso amor;
que si significa piedra,
en piedras hace señal
el arado de tus flechas.
(1024)

With this marriage and the birth of a child to Boaz and Ruth, Tirso completes the biblical version of the story of Ruth.

Tirso has embodied the four cardinal virtues in Boaz, Ruth, and Naomi. They have been prudent in choosing the right means toward worthy ends; they have been temperate in restraining themselves from overindulgence; they have shown fortitude in facing danger and in being patient, persevering, and constant; they have demonstrated the virtue of justice by giving each man his own or his due. Justice, according to natural law, only prescribes the minimum obligations men have toward one another. The virtue that goes beyond justice and embodies the highest and noblest love, taking all men as brothers, is charity.[14] This virtue is part of man's social obligation, as Naomi, Ruth, and Boaz readily demonstrate in their respective roles in the play. According to natural law man is obliged to love his neighbor as himself, since his neighbors are created and loved by the same God who created him, and since they are destined to enjoy the same common good. His right to happiness is morally equal to that of all other men since he shares in the common human nature. Charity obliges man to aid others in distress; this tenet is exemplified by the actions of Ruth, Naomi, and Boaz.[15] These three characters, unlike Elimelech and his sons, have chosen the right means toward worthy ends in giving help to those less fortunate than themselves. In contrast to Elimelech, they demonstrate prudence by moderating their human drives toward preservation of self and race. They have avoided the excessive indulgence and love of worldly goods to which Elimelech and his sons fell victim, and instead have given to the poor, recognizing this act as a social obligation. Boaz and Ruth are in a special way an affirmative part of God's plan and have set an example by conforming to the norm of morality and to natural law in their dealings with society. Natural law holds that man as a social being abhors solitude and desires companionship. It likewise holds that it is obvious by man's acts that he is impelled to live in the company of his fellow man and to cooperate with him in society for common ends. Since man cannot supply his basic needs by himself, he turns by nature to his fellow man. Through Naomi, Ruth, Boaz, and the peasants, one can readily see that man is naturally suited for society and is impelled to join his fellow man. Neither the peasant nor the landlord can exist alone; they are mutually dependent. The economic aspects and functions of society are repeatedly stressed in the play, especially by the peasants. Society as the Scholastics defined it was an order through which an enduring union of persons, bound morally under authority, cooperate for a common good. The social order maintains an opportunity for its members to act in a communal spirit and thereby increases the powers of individuals through mutual supplementation. Given its authority by natural law, society is a means to an end—man's happiness. God does not will the end, perfect happiness, without willing the means necessary to that end.

The poetic justice in *La mejor espigadera* rewards those who have lived in accordance with natural law, applying its principles to specific situations and as a result participating in the eternal law in a special way—by being provident for themselves and for others. It punishes those who have avoided their social obligations and have embraced worldly goods instead of spiritual ones. Thus Tirso has glossed the biblical text in order to set forth a basic ethical problem and to present his audience with exemplary characters who act in accordance with God's law by fulfilling their social obligations. In *La mejor espigadera* morally correct human behavior, which embraces brotherly love, is interpreted as the basis for the metaphysical harmony between man and God.

Chapter Four

The Auto Sacramental

In Golden Age drama the best expression of natural law is found in the *autos sacramentales* of Calderón. Because these works are frequently misunderstood by critic and layman alike, it might be well to examine the nature of this type of drama before considering specific examples of natural law in three of Calderón's *autos*.[1]

The *auto sacramental*, which stems from medieval liturgical drama,[2] begins to take form in the sixteenth century, and reaches its maturity as a genre with Calderón. Since there are almost no primary texts, it is difficult to determine the extent of the medieval theater in Spain. The first liturgical dramas to appear in the vulgar tongue were miracle plays, which flourished in the thirteenth and fourteenth centuries. These works dramatized legends and the miraculous intervention of the Virgin or the saints in human affairs. Mystery plays, popular in the fifteenth century, dramatized themes taken from the life of Christ and from the Bible. They did not use religious doctrine as the main topic to be demonstrated, nor did they teach dogma by means of drama as did the *autos sacramentales*. The type of religious play most like the *auto* was the morality play, which treated ethical problems not easily solved by religious doctrines. These plays were allegorical, and their primary purpose was moral guidance. On the basis of the medieval religious drama with which modern literary critics are familiar, it would seem that the *auto sacramental* took its material from the mysteries and its form from the moralities.[3] The *auto* should not, however, be considered a mere renewal or continuation of either the mysteries or the moralities. The eucharistic theme found in most of the *autos sacramentales* and their use as public acts of worship in the Corpus Christi feast differentiate them from the earlier dramatic forms.[4]

The *autos sacramentales* were magnificent spectacles, with splendid decoration, scenery, costumes, and music; they were performed throughout Spain as an integral part of the Corpus Christi feasts. The procession which was part of this cheerful feast was very colorful. First came the figure of the *Tarasca*, a dragon-like serpent with a woman riding on its back.[5] This was followed by men and women performing folk dances, children singing hymns, and several *gigantones*, huge Moorish or Negro figures. Then, amid angels playing musical instruments, people bearing candles, and singers, came the bishop and priests bearing the Holy Eucharist beneath a canopy. Finally came the decorated *carros* carrying the actors from the various public theaters who were going to perform on this occasion. Special platform stages (*tablados*) were built at several points in the city, and the *carros* were grouped around these stages. *Comisarios* appointed by the city selected the theatrical managers (*autores*) whose companies would represent the *autos*. These *autores* were required to give trial performances for the *comisarios* before finally presenting the plays at the Eucharistic feast.

According to Lope, the *auto sacramental* was a dramatic piece which should glorify the Holy Eucharist at a public spectacle, thereby exalting the faith and combating the errors of the heretics.[6] Calderón broadened the anti-Reformation spirit of the *autos* of Lope, Valdivielso, and Tirso into a profound study of dogma in order to glorify the faith. One can readily see the close relationship between the *autos sacramentales* of Calderón and the Corpus Christi spectacle in his definition, found in the *auto, La segunda esposa y triunfar muriendo:*

LABRADOR.   Mas decidme, aquellas torres,
o triunfales carros, que
el aire ocupan disformes,
¿para qué fin aquí están?

PASTOR.   A fin de hacer las mejores
fiestas que pudo la idea
inventar.

LABRADOR.   ¿Qué son?

PASTOR.   Sermones
puestos en verso, en idea
representable, cuestiones
de la Sacra Teología
que no alcanzan mis razones

a explicar ni comprender,
y el regocijo dispone
en aplauso deste día.[7]

In Calderón's view, the *autos sacramentales* were dramatized sermons whose subjects were *cuestiones de la Sacra Teología* and whose purpose was the *aplauso deste día*. As a part of the Corpus Christi feast they were meant to teach and to entertain the multitude by bringing complex theological instruction as well as spectacle to the *tablado*.

Calderón foresaw adverse criticism of his *autos* because of their content and style. He answers his future critics in a prologue to the *Autos sacramentales alegóricos y historiales* published in 1677, entitled "Anticipadas disculpas a las objecciones que pueden ofrecerse a la impresión destos autos." Anticipating that some readers would be annoyed by the appearance of the same characters in many *autos*, he explains that since the *asunto* was always the same he had no choice but to use the same means to express it.

Habrá quien haga fastidioso reparo de ver que en los más de estos Autos están introducidos unos mismos personajes como son: la Fe, la Gracia, la Culpa, la Naturaleza, el Judaísmo, la Gentilidad, etcétera. A que se satisface, o se procura satisfacer, con que siendo siempre uno mismo el asunto, es fuerza caminar a su fin con unos mismos medios, mayormente si se entra en consideración de que estos mismos medios, tantas veces repetidos, siempre van a diferente fin en su argumento, con que, a mi corto juicio, más se le debe dar estimación que culpa a este reparo, que el mayor primor de la naturaleza es que con unas mismas facciones haga tantos rostros diferentes, con cuyo ejemplar, ya que no sea primor, sea disculpa el haber hecho tantos diferentes Autos con unos mismos personajes.[8]

He reminds us that these plays were meant to be seen once a year, not read in succession, and tells us that the *autos* lose much of their effect when they are read unless the reader is able to supply the missing elements through his imagination: "Parecerán tibios algunos trozos; respecto de que el papel no puede dar de sí ni lo sonoro de la música, ni lo aparatoso de las tramoyas, y si ya no es que el que lea haga en su imaginación composición de lugares, considerando lo que sería sin entero juicio de lo que es, que muchas veces descaece el que escribe de sí mismo por conveniencias del pueblo y del tablado.[9] Calderón was not always able to write as he had wished, since, as he points out, he had to consider the public and the requirements of the stage and since the religious nature of the Corpus Christi feast was necessarily limiting.[10]

The *auto sacramental*, with its theological and philosophical content, its symbols and its abstraction, has been the center of controversy, enduring exaggerated scorn or praise.[11] The climate of opinion of the Golden Age began to change at the end of the eighteenth century, and the *autos* were no longer held in esteem. The neoclassic world was quite remote from the milieu which had produced the *auto sacramental*. In a chapter dedicated to critics of the *auto*, Professor Parker includes some of their attacks. Blas Antonio Nasarre condemns the *autos sacramentales* for "la interpretación cómica de las Sagradas Escrituras, llenas de alegorías y metáforas violentas, de anacronismos horribles; y lo peor es, mezclando y confundiendo lo sagrado con lo profano." Nicolás Moratín delivers a typically neoclassical attack on the *autos'* lack of verisimilitude, asking, "¿Es posible que hable la Primavera? ¿Ha oido usted en su vida una palabra al Apetito? ¿Sabe usted cómo es el metal de voz de la Rosa?"[12] Neoclassical literary taste, which condemned the *autos* for their failure to conform to its own theory of drama, brought about their prohibition from the stage in 1765.[13]

The general characteristic of nineteenth-century critics is emotion; they either exalted or condemned the *autos* on the basis of their religious and philosophical content without regard to their dramatic art. As Ramón Silva suggests, these critics can be charged with provincialism:

The atmosphere of the nineteenth century was hardly propitious to appreciation of what Donne calls "the three-piled Papestry of Spain" and its representative dramatist. In the main, our criticism during that period assumes an attitude which damns with faint praise. It attempts to admire the art while condemning the religion which elicited it and refuses to recognize an objective historical fact which is fundamental to an understanding of the "Poet of Romanism." The strength of religious feeling in Spain, its pervasion of all aspects of Spanish life, and its expression in ways which to the stranger might seem impious were fatal to its just appraisal. The purely meridional concept of religion is offensive to many even to-day; by members of Protestant schools of criticism it was deemed superstitious, unprogressive and fanatical: one of them, indeed Sismondi, unable to comprehend a creed not his own, went so far as to condemn Calderón out of hand as the "poet of the Inquisition." British critics while somewhat more accommodating have gone for their inspiration mainly to the same source: hence the unsatisfactory nature of their judgments.[14]

Menéndez Pelayo, the giant of Spanish scholarship, attacked the *autos* in his *Calderón y su teatro*, published in 1881. Although he modified his judgments in the 1911 edition of the work, his criticism condemned Calderón to relative obscurity for years because many readers both in and out of Spain followed without question the dictates of this powerful scholar. Professor Wardropper deals with this problem in a forthright manner: "It is customary for critics, when writing about a play by Calderón, to bow reverentially in the direction of the late Marcelino Menéndez Pelayo. . . . It is forgotten that Spaniards despise Calderón precisely because of their exaggerated respect for Menéndez Pelayo's critical judgment. . . . This idolatry of a critic— particularly of such an incompetent critic—impairs the health of Calderón studies, and of Spanish studies in general."[15] Although Wardropper's opinions may seem exaggerated to some, I agree with him when he says that hispanists have mistaken positivism for literary criticism. "I have maintained that Menéndez Pelayo's criticism is considerably inferior to his erudition, that it is in fact worthless. It is as a positivistic scholar, not as a critic, that we should remember him. His criticism should have been dismissed from the start. It is our fault if we mistake the accumulation of data for a sign of literary intelligence."[16] Wardropper believes that it is principally the British scholars who refuted Menéndez Pelayo's judgment and brought about the revived popularity of Calderón.[17] The *autos sacramentales* have been restored to their rightful position in Spanish literature principally through the efforts of Alexander A. Parker and the Spanish critic Ángel Valbuena Prat. Both Valbuena and Parker have emphasized the necessity of understanding the allegorical form and the doctrinal content of the *autos*. As they suggest, many readers are not able to comprehend the *autos sacramentales* fully because of their unfamiliarity with the subject matter or because of the abstractness of the form.

To understand the content of the *autos*, it is necessary to have some knowledge of the doctrine of transubstantiation which was the object of study in many European universities during the seventeenth century, for this dogma is an important element of Calderón's *autos*. Parker analyzes the *asunto* of the *auto sacramental* and its relationship to the *argumento* clearly and concisely:

The *asunto* of every *auto* is . . . the Eucharist, but the *argumento* can vary from one to another: it can be any "historia divina"—historical, legendary, or fictitious—provided that it throws some light on some aspect of the *asunto*. One should give very careful qualifications, therefore, when stating that the Eucharist is the exclusive "theme" of the *autos*, and one should not jump, as Fitzmaurice-Kelly did, to the *a priori* conclusion that the *auto*'s "range is, therefore, extremely limited"; for the fact is that the range is very extensive indeed. The wider variation possible in the *argumentos* depends upon the number of aspects in the *asunto* capable of illustration.[18]

These plays, as a part of the Corpus Christi feast, were written and presented in honor of the Eucharist. No other doctrine of the Church could have served Calderón better as an *asunto* for his *autos sacramentales*. As Professor Parker points out: "Of all Catholic dogmas the doctrine of the Eucharist is the one that can offer the widest scope to the theological dramatist. So all-embracing is it, so central to the whole theological system, that there is hardly a single dogma that cannot, in a sense, be included in it. So central is it also to the spiritual life of the Catholic that any aspect of ethical doctrine can be made to bear on it. For his *argumentos* the dramatist can therefore draw on virtually the whole wide field of Catholic dogmatic and moral theology."[19] Calderón had a broad knowledge of the Church Fathers, the Bible, and scholastic philosophy, from which he derived the themes of his *autos*.[20] Many of these themes, such as Original Sin, the Incarnation, and the Redemption, can be related to the Eucharist; thus the treatment of this sacrament in the *autos sacramentales* can vary extensively according to the nature of the allegory employed.

Calderón's use of allegory gives him freedom to treat history, legends, mythology, scripture, and moral philosophy in an exegetical manner, and enables him to present complex philosophical and theological ideas to his audience. Abstract concepts become visible dramatic representations, as he explains:

> Y pues lo caduco no
> puede comprender lo eterno,
> y es necesario que para
> venir en conocimiento
> suyo haya un medio visible,
> que en el corto caudal nuestro
> del concepto imaginado
> pase a práctico concepto.[21]

The *concepto imaginado* which treats *lo eterno* becomes the *práctico concepto* through the dramatic action, which is an extended metaphor. Calderón further explains his use of allegory in accommodating his ideas to the demands of the stage.

> Y pues ya la fantasía
> ha entablado el argumento,
> entable la realidad
> la metáfora. . . .[22]

While it is the imagination that produces the *argumento*, it is the metaphor that presents the physical reality on the stage. The meaning of imagination (*fantasía*), as understood by Calderón, comes from Aquinas.[23] According to Thomas the imagination dematerializes concrete images, forming phantasms which enable man to retain knowledge by reproducing and associating things sensed. It has a creative function which consists in making composite sensory images from various details of past experiences which it retains. For the artist, the imagination is a more important power than his external senses. While he must have acute powers of observation, it is more important for him to have a keen imagination so that he may make good use of these observations. Referring to Thomas Aquinas's theory of imagination and how it is related to that of Calderón, Parker states:

This theory of the imagination shows us clearly why Calderón constantly uses the term to explain dramatic technique. Firstly, the world of imagination is unlimited, it is a kind of "dream-world" unhampered by time or place, including all possibilities and impossibilities. Hence the material it offers for an *argumento* is unrestricted by any consideration of verisimilitude. . . . Secondly, the imagination presents the reflecting mind with the picture it requires in order to understand an idea, and with the diagram it requires in order to communicate it by means of illustration or analogy. Thus the mind transforms the concept with which theology furnishes it into a mental picture which fixes it (*concepto imaginado*), and then, in order to communicate the concept to other minds, it makes use of this mental picture which, through the technical resources of the stage, is turned into a dramatic picture and endowed with movement (*práctico concepto*).[24]

The allegorical dramatic action is the medium which presents the idea as a concrete expression of reality on the stage. Professor Parker points out that for Calderón there is another very important level of reality which relates to allegory, and that this other level of reality is very important in understanding the *autos sacramentales:* "Allegory is the link between two different planes of 'reality': on the one hand there is the visible reality of the stage, on the other the invisible reality of the order of beings of which the stage-action is only the representation or reflection. In relation to the audience's vision the action is 'real,' but in relation to the reality that it mirrors it is 'unreal.'"[25] The spectator thus experiences the visible reality before him on the stage and participates in ontological reality; hence life could be thought of as a dream and the dreams could be dreams. A very important function of Calderón's *autos* is to mirror ontological reality, making the themes that he uses metaphysically and theologically true. Characters, costumes, dialogue, stage directions, music, and histrionics all help to serve the same end—to transform the *conceptos imaginados* through allegory into *prácticos conceptos* which could be readily understood by the audience.[26]

Calderón organized his thought in patterns consistent with the philosophy and preoccupations of seventeenth-century Spain, which was experiencing a powerful regeneration of scholastic philosophy. The most debated question concerning the philosophical influences in Calderón's *autos* is whether he is predominantly a Thomist or an Augustinian. Some scholars, Margraff in particular, point out Calderón's close affiliation with the philosophy of Augustine.[27] The more important critics of the *autos*, however, admit the greater influence of scholastic philosophers, and especially of Thomas Aquinas.[28] Ángel Valbuena Prat believes that Calderón is predominantly a neo-Thomist influenced by Jesuits such as Suárez and his contemporaries.[29] But Calderón was a dramatist, not a philosopher, and as such he did not follow any one particular system of philosophy to the exclusion of all others. Incorporating the tenets and terminology of the Scholastics in his *autos*, Calderón was able to communicate his ideas to the audience in a very logical manner, using allegory to transform philosophical doctrines into dramatic concepts. He was, as Parker observes, an eclectic, taking that which best suited his purpose for each particular *auto*.[30] However, because of its intimate relation to various themes, Thomistic-Aristotelian doctrine in the form of natural-law ethics, so fundamental to the climate of opinion of Golden Age Spain, is the single most coherent body of philosophical thought in the *autos sacramentales*, and as such it must be taken into consideration for an understanding of the *autos* in their profundity.

Chapter Five

El gran teatro del mundo

Calderón emphasizes theology in some of his *autos* while in others he stresses moral philosophy. *El gran teatro del mundo* and *No hay más fortuna que Dios* both emphasize philosophical rather than theological problems in their treatment of the restlessness of man in this world. In *No hay más fortuna que Dios* Calderón dramatizes the ethical problem of man's use of goods in his pursuit of happiness and how this use leads him either to accept or to reject God's providence. *El gran teatro del mundo* deals with a similar ethical problem, but emphasizes man's moral conduct on the individual level—*obra bien, que Dios es Dios* and on the social level—*ama al otro como a ti.*[1] In this *auto*, through the comparison of life to drama, Calderón attempts to explain man's anguish as he is confronted with his involuntary presence in the world.[2] Alexander A. Parker believes that the idea of life as drama is not the theme, but rather the allegory of this *auto*. In his profound analysis of the play Parker concludes that the portrayal of human life in *El gran teatro del mundo* is in terms of social classes and that the play itself is sociological rather than philosophical in its analysis of these social classes in relation to each other and in its treatment of the ultimate goal of human existence. Concerning the precise theme of the *auto* he says: "This takes the form of an analysis of human life in terms of social classes: an analysis of the relation of social classes to each other and to the final end of human existence, and of the nature of a moral life in terms of individual social status. It is thus not primarily a 'philosophical' but a 'sociological' *auto*."[3] Ángel Valbuena Prat suggests that *El gran teatro del mundo* is *filosófico-moral*, but fails to develop this interesting idea.

La doctrina del orden social, precedente de Santo Tomás de Aquino, y concordante con el pensamiento de los teólogos españoles de los

siglos XVI y XVII, rige la acción de la comedia de la vida, y A. A.
Parker ha estudiado este aspecto con notoria penetración. Con todo,
creo es excesivo llamar al Auto "sociológico." La fusión de la idea de
"teatro" y "mundo" es la fundamental, aunque en esa excelsa
comedia sea la ley social, el orden que la hace conforme a la idea
dispuesta por el Autor. Como lo teórico no empece a lo práctico, la
denominación exacta, y de acuerdo con la terminología de la época
sería la de "Auto filosófico-moral."[4]

I would agree with Professor Parker that the *auto* is sociological, but
only to the extent that it considers man as a social being. To apply
the term "sociological" to a Golden Age play may be misleading
because we use this adjective to describe the interrelationships
between men in society in a scientific and amoral way. There is
nothing either scientific or amoral about the climate in which
Calderón's Autor can create a stage, people it with actors, and then
judge the merits of individual performances. This *auto sacramental* is
not primarily sociological in the modern or scientific sense, but
filosófico-moral, because its action elaborates an ethical problem
based on natural law which treats morality in human nature and in
society. In *El gran teatro del mundo* God, el Autor, has endowed the
characters with a will which is entirely free and which, consequently,
can be attracted to the apparent as well as to the real good. The
ethical problem facing them is the morally correct use of goods, both
in a social and in an individual sense, to satisfy their desires and to
bring them perfect happiness.

The structure of this play is simple and precise. In the first part of
the *auto sacramental* el Autor relates the purpose and nature of the
drama as an allegory of human life; the second part treats the
creation of man and the distribution of roles to the performers; the
third presents the drama of life itself with men as its actors, el
Mundo as both stage manager and theater, Grace as the prompter,
and, as the Author-Producer, God. Each actor portrays a person of a
particular station in human life as an individual and as a member of
society, thus the *auto* is given both metaphysical and ethical significance.

In the initial scene of *El gran teatro del mundo* el Autor gives stage
directions to el Mundo; these opening lines relate the creation and
the distribution of beauty. When asked why the world was created,

el Autor explains the *concepto imaginado* of the *auto sacramental.*

> Pues soy tu Autor, y tú mi hechura eres
> hoy, de un concepto mío
> la ejecución a tus aplausos fío.
>
> (203–04)

The world is to be a reflection of the will and intellect of el Autor. It is the Author's intention to create a *fiesta:*

> Una fiesta hacer quiero
> a mi mismo poder, si considero
> que solo a ostentación de mi grandeza
> fiestas hará la gran naturaleza;
> y como siempre ha sido
> lo que más ha alegrado y divertido
> la representación bien aplaudida,
> y es representación la humana vida,
> una comedia sea
> la que hoy el cielo en tu teatro vea.
>
> (204)

El Autor will give each man the part that will suit him, and el Mundo will fabricate *apariencias* and distribute the *trajes* to the actors. El Mundo, as intermediary between God and man, holds the goods which, as in the teachings of Aquinas, are to be the means to man's ultimate end.[5]

> Yo *el gran teatro del mundo,*
> para que en mí representen
> los hombres, y cada uno
> halle en mí la prevención
> que le impone el papel suyo,
> como parte obedencial,
> que solamente ejecuto
> lo que ordenas, que aunque es mía
> la obra el milagro es tuyo,
>
> (204)

In the first *jornada* of the drama of life, natural law is promulgated to man:

> En la primera jornada
> sencillo y cándido nudo
> de la gran ley natural,
> allá en los primeros lustros
> aparecerá un jardín
> con bellísimos dibujos,
> ingeniosas perspectivas,
> que se dude cómo supo
> la naturaleza hacer
> tan gran lienzo sin estudio.
>
> (204-05)

According to Aquinas, natural law, an expression of God's will, directs all actions and movements.[6] In the second *jornada* the written law is proclaimed so that man may be helped to find the path to his ultimate destiny.

> Acabado el primer acto,
> luego empezará el segundo
> *ley escrita* en que poner
> más apariencias procuro,
> pues para pasar a ella
> pasarán con pies enjutos
> los hebreos desde Egipto
> los cristales del mar rubio;
>
> . . . .
>
> Para salir con la ley
> Moisés a un monte robusto
> le arrebatará una nube
> en el rapto vuelo suyo.
>
> (205-06)

Aquinas teaches that while natural law is a moral and physical law, the Ten Commandments represent divine positive law imposed on man by God's direct revelation. These commandments, though they are statements of natural law, differ from it in the extent of promulgation, the Ten Commandments being decreed by external signs as divine positive law.[7] God further provides for man's attainment of his last end by bestowing upon him, through Grace, certain powers in order that he may have a further inclination toward supernatural good.[8]

> Y empezará la tercera
> jornada, donde hay anuncios
> que habrá mayores portentos
> por ser los milagros muchos
> de la *ley de gracia*, en que
> ociosamente discurro. (206)

The three laws oblige man to make his conduct conform to a norm of morality that will direct him to the ultimate end which God has created for him.[9] Thomas, in his definition of law, concludes by saying, "It is nothing else than an ordinance of reason for the common good, made by him who has care of the community, and promulgated."[10] Law in its proper sense serves the common good, is knowable, and is authoritative in its source. The function of divine law is to direct man to his last end without destroying his free will.

The dialogue between el Mundo and el Autor explains the divine plan of God's creation. El Mundo then distributes the benefits and burdens, which are equal essentially and different accidentally. These will be the instruments man will use to participate in the divine plan; the world will be filled with physical or apparent goods and moral or true goods, all of which will be at man's disposal.[11] Each character in *El gran teatro del mundo* has the purpose of attaining his final end, and he ought to accomplish this as an individual (*obra bien, que Dios es Dios*) and as a member of society (*ama al otro como a ti*). This is an obligation imposed on man by divine law, since he is equipped with an intellect with which to know this law and a will with which to obey it. If man fails to attain his ultimate goal, it will not be el Mundo's fault, but his own, since the human being is provided with the means to attain his last end. God anticipates man's confusion concerning divine justice and reminds him that life on earth is a drama:

> Aquello es representar,
> aunque piense que es vivir.
> Pero yo, Autor soberano,

sé bien qué papel hará
mejor cada uno; así va
repartiéndolos mi mano.
.   .   .   .
Justicia distributiva
soy, y *sé* lo que os conviene.

(207-08)

Although it may seem otherwise to man, the distributive justice of el
Autor is fair; each man has that which he needs to act out his role in
the play. El Autor then advises the actors to be ready to end their
parts at any hour, since they will be held responsible at all times for
their every act.

Para eso, común grey,
tendré desde el pobre rey
para enmendar al que errare
y enseñar al que ignorare
con el apunto a mi Ley;
ella a todos os dirá
lo que habéis de hacer, y así
nunca os quejaréis de mí.
Albedrío tenéis ya . . .

(209)

The law of God has been clearly enough promulgated so that the
creature will have a natural inclination to his proper end. The
individual then applies the norm of morality established by natural
law to his own acts by use of his own conscience. The general
principles—*obra bien* and *ama al otro*—are self-evident to man
through natural law,[12] but this law does not tell him whether a
particular act done by a particular person is morally correct or not.
Man alone has the ability to apply the law to specific concrete
situations; his conscience is the link between natural law and the
individual act, and it is this faculty which allows man to make
practical judgments. Thus the sufficient knowledge which man
receives through his reason makes him responsible for his conduct.
All the characters of the drama know what parts they are to play and
all are given natural reason; hence they have an equal opportunity to
comply with God's law and attain happiness. Following Thomistic

theory, the role of each character in the play represents his participation in eternal law.[13] God guides man to his ultimate end, and the
world gives man all that is necessary, including natural law and its
self-evident principles, to reach this end. All of the characters through
use of will and intellect can satisfy their every desire if they perform
their parts well.

In addition to the natural gifts which el Autor gives man, el
Mundo provides vestments for the characters. El Rey, el Rico, la
Hermosura and la Discreción are satisfied with their roles; el Niño,
who dies before being born, is resigned to act his short part, but el
Pobre and el Labrador are disappointed with their status because they
cannot understand the mystery of God's distributive justice. Thus
begins *la gran comedia de la vida*, with some men happy with what
they believe to be benefits and others dissatisfied with what they
think are burdens. The action of the play will dramatize man's role in
the social order. This role should be a preparation for the eternal life,
but because man judges that worldly goods are eternal, his part takes
on the nature of a dream from which he must awaken. The twofold
purpose of man's existence—individual and social—is made known to
him by la Ley de Gracia:

> Yo, que Ley de Gracia soy,
> la fiesta introduzgo hoy;
> para enmendar al que yerra
> en este papel se encierra
> la gran comedia, que Vos
> compusisteis solo en dos
> versos que dicen así:
> (*Canta.*)
> "Ama al otro como a ti,
> y obra bien, que Dios es Dios."
> (211)

In the last two lines the norm of morality is established for man,
who now has a standard by which to gauge his conduct as a social
being.[14] Through the use of his intellect, man is able to know the
proximate norm of morality, which is right reason, and the ultimate
norm, which is eternal law. God directs all things to their ends by the
nature he gives them; therefore man's conduct is right if it conforms

to natural law and wrong if it does not. In the commands *ama al otro como a ti* and *obra bien, que Dios es Dios*, the norm of morality both on the social and on the individual level is made known to man in order that he attain his last end and help other men secure theirs.[15]

As the drama of life begins, each character presents a social problem and an attitude of life. The ethical problem is the use of worldly goods correctly as a means leading to God rather than as an end. La Discreción has a morally healthy attitude toward the gifts she has received, as is evident in the question which she poses to el Mundo:

> ¿Qué haré yo para emplear
> bien mi ingenio?
>
> (212)

La Hermosura, who believes that her beauty is an end in itself, asks:

> ¿Qué haré yo
> para lograr mi hermosura?
>
> (212)

El Rico, so intensely interested in himself and in his property, is devoured by egoism, and consequently his question is:

> ¿Qué haré yo para ostentar
> mi riqueza?
>
> (213)

El Labrador, dissatisfied with his role of having to provide food for his fellow man, intends rather to use his goods for his own selfish ends:[16]

> Con esto un Nabal-Carmelo
> seré de aquesta región
> y me habrán menester todos,
> pero muy hinchado yo,
> entonces, ¿qué podré hacer?
>
> (212–13)

El Pobre, like la Discreción, is morally healthy, asking only how he may survive:

¿Qué haré yo
para sufrir mis desdichas?
(213)

El Rey, the last to appear, basks in his own worldly goods, the temporal power of his empire. His question is:

¿Qué he menester yo en el mundo?
(213)

The first scene of the drama, in which the characters are trying to make beneficial use of the goods distributed to them, ends with la Ley answering each question with the moral warning, *obrar bien, que Dios es Dios*. Only two characters, la Discreción and el Pobre, are conforming readily to this command in their conduct.

The second scene of the drama of life revolves around el Pobre, whose role is to stimulate the virtue of charity in the other characters.

El labrador, si cansado
viene del campo, ya halló
honesta mesa su hambre
si opulenta mesa no;
al rico le sobra todo;
y solo, en el mundo, yo
hoy de todos necesito,
y así llegó a todos hoy,
porque ellos viven sin mí
pero yo sin ellos no.
(213)

Poverty is the good upon which the virtue of *caritas* depends, and as such it stands at the center of action in this second scene, motivating the characters to love one another as they love themselves. El Pobre asks each one of the characters for alms and receives a variety of answers. La Hermosura, so interested in self-esteem, does not even hear him. El Rico hears, but refuses to give him anything:

¿No hay puertas donde llamar?
¿Así os entráis donde estoy?

En el umbral del zaguán
pudierais llamar, y no
haber illegado hasta aquí.

(213)

El Rey does not help el Pobre directly, saying:

Para eso tengo ya
mi limosnero mayor.

(214)

He does, however, help la Discreción (who represents the Church) by
sustaining her when she falls into his arms. El Labrador sees in el
Pobre his own greatest fault, laziness, and in a comical scene offers
the beggar his *azadón*.

¿No tenéis vergüenza
que un hombrazo como vos
pida? ¡Servid, noramala!
No os andéis hecho un bribón.
Y si os falta que comer,
tomad aqueste azadón
con que lo podéis ganar.

(214)

In their failure to be charitable, the characters show a lack of social
conscience. La Discreción offers el Pobre bread, saying, "Tomad, y
dadme perdón" (214); but with this one exception, the characters
have in varying degrees abdicated their responsibility for their fellow
men by not performing their moral duty as social beings. They have
not loved one another as they love themselves and are allowed to
commit this moral error by el Autor, who exclaims:

Yo, bien pudiera enmendar
los yerros que viendo estoy;
pero por eso les di
albedrío superior
a las pasiones humanas,
por no quitarles la acción
de merecer con sus obras.

(214)

La Ley again warns the characters to live morally correct lives:

> (*Canta.*) Obrar bien, que Dios es Dios.
> (*Recita.*)
> A cada uno por sí
> y a todos juntos, mi voz
> ha advertido; ya con esto
> su culpa será su error
> (*Canta.*)
> Ama al otro como a ti
> y obrar bien que Dios es Dios.
> (214)

At this point in the play the theme of *La danza de la muerte* is introduced, and all of the characters are given the opportunity to repent before their worldly goods are taken away from them by death. The king is summoned by la Voz, who says:

> Rey de este caduco imperio,
> cese, cese tu ambición
> que en el teatro del mundo
> ya tu papel se acabó.
> (215)

The king, believing in his earthly glory, has distorted his role in the play, but does beg for forgiveness for his errors in these last moments of his life. La Hermosura ignores the existence of a macrocosm, believing that her power is greater even than that of the king, since her empire reigns in the soul of the microcosm—man.

> Luego infiero
> con causa que mi imperio es el primero,
> pues que reina en las almas la hermosura.
> 'Pequeño mundo' la filosofía
> llamó al hombre; si en él mi imperio fundo,
> como el cielo lo tiene, como el suelo,
> bien puede presumir la deidad mía
> que el que al hombre llamó 'pequeño mundo,'
> llamará a la mujer 'pequeño cielo.'
> (215)

In her misuse of the good distributed to her, la Hermosura has led men astray rather than to God, and she leaves the stage wishing that she had acted her part in a better manner. When la Voz summons el Labrador, he asks for more time to leave his land in a good state, so that it will be productive for those who will follow him. He has realized that his role in society is to provide food for others and has shown charity for those who will succeed him. Thus, ending his part as well as he can, el Labrador repents. El Rico realizes that his role is almost finished, but he is so lost in worldly goods that he alone cannot reach the point of repentance:

> Pues si tan breve se nombra,
> de nuestra vida gocemos
> el rato que la tenemos:
> dios a nuestro vientre hagamos.
> ¡Comamos hoy y bebamos,
> que mañana moriremos!
>
> (217)

El Pobre awaits his call to death morally prepared, as does la Discreción; both have lived their lives with the proper end in mind. Thus society comes to an end on stage as el Mundo collects the costumes from the characters. All are now essentially equal. El Autor then appears, and metes out justice to the actors: El Pobre and la Discreción join el Autor; la Hermosura, el Rey, and el Labrador, who died repentant, go to Purgatory; el Niño remains in Limbo, and el Rico is condemned to Hell. The characters have been divested of all material goods, for these belong to the world; they retain only their *buenas obras*.

> No te puedo quitar las buenas obras.
> . . . .
> Ya es tarde; que en muriendo, no os asombre,
> no puede ganar méritos el hombre.
> Ya que he cobrado augustas majestades,
> ya que he borrado hermosas perfecciones,
> ya que he frustrado altivas vanidades,
> ya que he igualado cetros y azadones;
> al teatro pasad de las verdades,
> que éste el teatro es de las ficciones.
>
> (220)

Each has been judged according to the degree that he has followed the basic tenets of natural law—*obra bien* and *ama al otro como a ti*. The enigma of existence in society is that man is confronted by forces which he can neither comprehend fully nor control, yet he is responsible through the use of intellect and will for his moral situation. The proper object of intellect is truth; but man, being a finite and fallible rational being, may make erroneous judgments which, when presented to the will, cause him to choose the apparent rather than the true good. In *El gran teatro del mundo*, for those who have chosen earthly existence and material goods as ends in themselves, death is humiliation; but for those who know these things to be intermediate ends and who have held true to the norm of morality through the right use of reason, death is willingly accepted because it leads to eternal happiness. Thus this *auto sacramental* is not primarily sociological but *filosófico-moral* in that the *concepto imaginado* of the play is an ethical problem based on moral philosophy.

Chapter Six

No hay más fortuna que Dios

In *No hay más fortuna que Dios* Calderón uses ethical themes based on natural law to such an extent that without a knowledge of the philosophical content of this *auto sacramental*, it would be extremely difficult to understand it. *No hay más fortuna que Dios* treats an ethical problem which pertains to a fundamental precept of natural law—man's use of good in his pursuit of happiness leads him either to accept or to reject God's providence.

The doctrine of providence was one of the main apologetic themes of the Reformation and Counter-Reformation periods, while the role of fortune diminished and human conduct came to be explained in terms of free choices and divine purposes. In this *auto* Calderón is not interested in defining a metaphysical doctrine of providence, but rather in dramatizing human conduct in order to affirm the existence of divine purpose, distributive justice, and free will in life.

The ideas of fate, fortune, and providence are complex, and Calderón usually follows Aquinas in his treatment of them. Augustine and Aquinas agree in their thoughts concerning fate; both hold that nothing happens by chance.[1] While Thomas contends that divine providence imposes necessity upon some things, he believes that other things happen by contingency according to the nature of their proximate causes.[2] This does not mean that anything happens outside of God's providence; it means that certain effects willed by God happen contingently because God has prepared contingent causes for them.[3] Aquinas does allow for a kind of chance, stating that fate considered in regard to secondary causes is changeable, but that it acquires a certain unchangeableness from its being subject to divine providence.[4]

Calderón emphasizes the idea of God as an efficient cause, while still preserving the theory that man also is a cause of what happens to him. There are two realms of authority concerning human acts, God's and man's. The jurisdiction of man is subsidiary to that of

God. The dramatist, following Aquinas's ideas concerning man's power over his acts, holds that unless man makes good use of his intellect and will, he may fall victim to the power of fate.

A second philosophical doctrine basic to *No hay más fortuna que Dios* is man's pursuit of happiness. Calderón holds in common with Thomas the teleological view that there exists a highest good for man, something for which he constantly strives and which gives meaning to his life. According to natural law man acts for goals or ends; even if one tries to prove this idea wrong, he has an end in mind. No activity is possible except for the attainment of an end and for the sake of a good.[5] The intention or end becomes the first thing that stimulates the intellect; the execution or means is used to obtain the end. Explaining the order of intention (end) and execution (means) Aquinas says:

Now there is to be observed a twofold order in ends,—the order of intention, and the order of execution: and in either of these orders there must be something first. For that which is first in the order of intention, is the principle, as it were, moving the appetite; consequently, if you remove this principle, there will be nothing to move the appetite. On the other hand, the principle in execution is that wherein operation has its beginning; and if this principle be taken away, no one will begin to work. Now the principle in the intention is the last end; while the principle in execution is the first of the things which are ordained to the end. Consequently, on neither side is it possible to go on to infinity; since if there were no last end, nothing would be desired, nor would any action have its term, nor would the intention of the agent be at rest; while if there is no first thing among those that are ordained to the end, none would begin to work at anything, and counsel would have no term, but would continue indefinitely.[6]

The last end, for Thomas, is the first thing desired; if there were no ultimate end, nothing would be desired and there would not be any activity. He further asserts that there can be only one last end for all mankind. Many alternative ends would leave man dissatisfied, searching for other ends. Aquinas believes that all things desire their own perfection and that for this reason man seeks his ultimate and most perfect good.[7] Natural law holds that human conduct derives its moral goodness from the last end, and that men are morally good if their acts lead them to this last end and happiness. Happiness, the result of desire fulfilled by a state of satisfaction through possession of some good, is a guiding force for man's activity. The attainment of perfect happiness for man depends on the existence of a God and an immortal soul, since it is to be found only in the next world. Natural law deduces that man has a natural desire, given to him by God, for all the happiness he is capable of. If such a desire has been implanted by God it must be attainable, since God intends natural desires for fulfillment, not frustration. Man is held responsible for his acts in his attempt to attain this happiness, since through his natural reason he can and must judge what things are good for him. However, since man is fallible and finite, his judgments are subject to error and he may mistake the apparent good for the true good in his quest for happiness. It is this search and its implications which are at the core of the ethical problem dramatized in *No hay más fortuna que Dios*. The main action treats the moral use of goods while the background action (which becomes more important in the final scenes) deals with providence.

In Golden Age Spain one of the moral uses of the theater was to present virtues and vices through dramatic action. In *No hay más fortuna que Dios*, as in some other *autos sacramentales* of Calderón, the Devil appears in a prologue in which he explains the ideas that will later take the form of dramatic action.[8] Demonio sets the stage for man as he proclaims the doctrine of original sin, writing on the tree of good and evil:[9]

> Rásguese de ese tronco
> la arrugada corteza,
> que fue al Hombre padrón vegetativo
> y en su cuaderno bronco
> la Gran Naturaleza,
> con aqueste puñal, verá que escribo:
> *(Escribe en el tronco.)*
> *Muerto, aquí yace vivo*
> *todo el Género Humano.*[10]

Calderón regards the doctrine of Original Sin as basic to man's imperfect status on earth and his relentless quest for happiness. Man's appetite, which ought to have led him to happiness, was the cause of his fall instead. Error in human judgment hindered him from fulfilling his goal and finding complete satisfaction. Demonio continues saying:

> No pequeña violencia,
> en no grande distancia,
> el despeño corrió de su delito,
> pues avaro de ciencia
> le dejó en ignorancia
> la primera lección de su apetito;
> y aunque fuese Infinito,
> por su Infinito Objeto;
> con todo, de mi injuria
> no apagada la furia,
> mayores ruinas suyas me prometo.
>
> (615)

La Malicia is then summoned by the Devil as an aide in frustrating la Justicia. The plan is to confuse man so that he will not understand the distributive justice of God, and thus will be discontented with his status on earth. The Devil is aware of the fact that he will not be able to hinder the will of God; he explains the plan of distributive justice:

> Ya sabes, Malicia, cuánto
> Dios, con Providencia suma,
> asiste a todo y que nada
> desampara y desayuna,
> haciendo que su Justicia
> a cada uno distribuya,
> desde la hormiga más vil,
> a la más noble criatura,
> lo que más le importa para
> que admita a honra y gloria suya
> el gracioso Don del Ser,
> que sin él no fuera nunca.
>
> (616)

According to natural law, distributive justice—the equal distribution of benefits and burdens—stems from the fundamental equality of men based on their common nature and destiny. Though men may be different and unequal accidentally, essentially they are considered to be the same, since they have the same last end and the same means of attaining that last end. Although man may complain about the inequality that he sees, through natural reason he should be able to recognize distributive justice. In this *auto*, however, because of his partial ignorance of God's law and his misuse of internal and external senses, man will misunderstand the natural order and will rebel against God's justice. Demonio explains:

> Pero como es tan sensible
> esta terrena, esta ruda
> carne y sangre, no a Dios siempre
> como a primer causa juzga;
> y así, en humanos afectos,
> viendo que al Ser le disgusta
> no ser lo que ser quisiera,
> anda a buscar la segunda.
>
> (616)

Through his ignorance man will reject providence, attributing the worldly beauty he sees to fortune. He will not comprehend justice since he will not understand the principle of the first cause, and consequently will come to worship secondary causes, as Demonio explains:

> Yo pretendo que la [hermosura] halle
> en una mentira, a cuya
> causa te llamé; porque
> tú, Malicia, la introduzcas
> a los mortales en sola
> una voz.
>
> (616)

Through worship of the false deity fortune, some of the characters will be grateful for their gifts while others will lament their hardships. They will not give thanks or complain to God since they will not recognize him as the first cause. Instead they will attribute the effects that they see to secondary causes and will use these secondary causes as ends rather than as means. This will bring about such confusion that they will ultimately be able to recognize neither the means nor the ends.

> Con que olvidados de Dios
> venturas y desventuras,
> siendo él la Causa de todas,
> no le conozca ninguna.
> (616)

The action of the play is the dramatization of the Devil's plan for the confusion of man. Demonio reveals his thoughts saying:

> Para este concepto, que es
> el asunto a que hoy se ajusta
> mi deseo, he imaginado,
> como dije, fingir una
> deidad, que el nombre equivoque
> de la siempre sabia, augusta
> distributiva Justicia,
> haciéndolos que presuman
> que de la Fortuna nace
> lo que halaga o lo que angustia.
> (616)

Such is the plan that he has devised to frustrate divine justice. Calderón will use the Devil's thought as the core of his dramatic material, and it will serve the dramatist as a vehicle for presenting theological ideas.

> Y siendo así que en los rumbos
> del humano Ser sin duda
> *no hay más fortuna que Dios,*
> he de hacer que no discurran
> en su deidad, previniendo
> que a esta fantasma confusa,
> a esta idea imaginada,
> ciego enigma y cifra oscura,
> den las gracias o las quejas
> del Bien o el Mal que los busca.
> (616)

Thus the Devil, in the prologue of this *auto*, sets the stage for the action which will take place. Man's search for happiness and some ethical problems resulting from this search will be the subject of the allegory. As a result of his failure to understand the divine plan man will rebel against God's justice, seeking pleasure and avoiding pain. He will make himself alone the judge of good and evil, and because of this his thoughts will confuse the means with the end. He will not know whether he should look for human fulfillment in earthly goods or whether he is capable of finding a lasting happiness at all. Man's conflicting desires and his confusion will be the cause of disordered love, as he searches for happiness in temporal goods rather than in God.

As the action of the play begins, the scene is set for man's quest for the good. The stage decorations include two *peñascos,* and two *árboles.* From the branches of the tree of good and evil hang the goods of distributive justice: *una corona de laurel, un cetro, un espejo, un libro, una espada, un bastón, una azada, un cayado* and *una Cruz* (617). At the foot of the tree, under the goods which they are to receive, sleep el Poder, la Hermosura, la Discreción,[11] la Milicia, el Pobre, and la Labranza. La Justicia Distributiva enters, singing the praise of God as she distributes the goods to the characters.

> Despertad a la vida, mortales,
> despertad, despertad a la vida,
> y admitiendo cada uno el Estado
> en que Dios quiere que nazca y que viva,
> las gracias le dad
> del bien que os envía,
> y nadie al nacer
> se alegre o se aflija,
> proque hasta la muerte
> no hay dicha o desdicha.
>
> (617)

The characters must awaken from their indeterminate condition of sleep; no action can take place until la Justicia distributes the goods which will remove this status of indetermination, allowing each being to act for an end. The distribution is just, since all of the characters are essentially equal although it may appear otherwise.

> En los Estados que ordeno
> veréis que a todos igualo,

pues ningún Estado es malo
como el Hombre en él sea bueno;
lleno de glorias o lleno
de penas nadie a otro pida,
pues son a entrada y salida,
nacer y morir, iguales.
(617)

La Justicia has implied the three presuppositions of natural-law ethics: the existence of God, the immortality of the soul, and the freedom of the will. No condition of man is bad. All men are equally endowed with a free will with which they may choose to act rightly or wrongly; thus all have the opportunity to seek and attain the highest good.

La Justicia soy, y yo,
sin ser liberal ni corta,
doy lo que a cada uno importa,
aunque él presuma que no.
Dios la experiencia dejó
de esto a su Juicio escondida.
Y así, para cuando os pida
la cuenta de Estados tales.
(618)

Because man has natural reason and is able to apply this to his experience, he will be held responsible for his actions. There is a definite moral code for him to obey. Man may not always think, however, that God is just in distributing goods; since his natural reason is limited he will not understand God's justice completely.

La Justicia Distributiva shakes the branches of the tree and the *insignias* fall into the hands of the characters for whom they are destined. El Poder is the first to awaken, with a *cetro* and *laurel* in his hands; la Labranza follows with an *azadón;* la Hermosura, with an *espejo;* la Milicia, with an *espada;* la Discreción, with a *libro;* and el Pobre, with a *báculo*. All of the characters are pleased with the benefits which they have received except la Labranza, who complains:

> ¡Qué triste! ¡Qué importuna
> suerte, sin piedad alguna,
> es la que mi Estado alcanza!
>
> (618)

and el Pobre, who laments:

> Pero ¿qué importa (¡ay de mí!)
> entre tantas penas una
> piedad? ¡Oh vida importuna!
> ¿Quién, dime, en tanta tristeza
> yo nazco a ser?
>
> (618)

The characters ask who distributed the goods and burdens among them. Malicia, the Devil's assistant, answers them implying that it was Fortuna: "Por quien bien o mal gozamos,/ nuestra Fortuna sigamos" (618).

At this time la Cruz appears to the characters, a gift which none of them agrees to accept. Justicia advises them to take the Cross in order to improve their status and to progress toward their ultimate end, explaining that it is a *don voluntario.*

> Aquese precioso don
> (otra vez a decir torno)
> para todos y ninguno
> viene ni ajeno ni propio.
> Para ninguno, porque
> habiendo albedrío, es notorio
> que no le da terminado
> el cielo al uno ni al otro;
> y para todos, porque
> si bien sus piedades noto,
> a ninguno se le niega.
>
> (619)

The supernatural order which is hidden in la Cruz seems mysterious and paradoxical to the characters. Because of their selfish motives they are content with their material goods and do not wish any burdens. If la Cruz is to be a burden to them, they cannot comprehend how it can also be a benefit. They decide to reject it and to follow fortune, failing to see the true good.

All things which they have received are ontologically good. According to Aquinas, every being, by the very fact that it exists, has some goodness about it. Ontologically a being is good for something in that it contributes to the harmony and perfection of the universe. Everything also has a certain degree of physical goodness. However, since not everything is good for every being, man must judge what things are good for him. As we see in *No hay más fortuna que Dios* these human judgments are open to error, since the characters mistake the apparent for the true good. Aquinas believes that if some lesser thing makes impossible the attainment of some greater good and especially of the highest good, then the lesser thing is not a true good for man. The problem which arises for the characters in *No hay más fortuna que Dios* is that the good which attracts the appetite is not always the moral good.

As the *auto* continues, the characters misuse the goods they have received: el Poder and la Hermosura endeavor to attain glory, la Milicia and la Discreción are prepared to accept the burdens of life only in order to satisfy their desire for fame, and el Pobre and la Labranza are satisfied merely to avoid further suffering and hardship. As opportunists who, because of their irrational conduct, live haphazardly, they do not concentrate on the highest good but are satisfied to confine themselves to the immediate goals, neglecting the remote ones. The characters in the play do not employ evil means in obtaining their goods. Their error is that they do not use natural goods correctly, as a means to the last end.

Calderón's concept of evil is introduced in the *auto* by the Devil:

> Común Mal de los mortales,
> que en los estados de todos
> mal hallados con sus suertes
> asistes.
>
> . . . .
>
> MALICIA.   . . .¿Qué pretendes, Lucero,
> de un Mal gustoso
> que, teniéndole muchos,
> le apartan pocos?

DEMONIO.   Que tú el rebozo te pongas,
pues que se quita el rebozo
(*Cúbrele con su capa*.)
el Bien para que a contrario
muestres, que desde el gozoso
estado al mísero estado,
si hay Bien en uno y en otro,
también hay Mal.

(621)

To comprehend the term *evil* as Calderón uses it, we must refer to the theory that evil does not exist in the positive sense.[12] Since no perfect good exists on earth, neither does any perfect happiness. There is a gradation of imperfect beings on earth; evil exists negatively in the ontological good insofar as this good is not perfect. This view may be better understood by considering Étienne Gilson's comments on evil: "Now every nature desires its own existence and its own perfection. The perfection and being, therefore, of every nature are truly goods. But if the being and perfection of all things are goods, then it follows that evil, which is the opposite of good, has neither perfection nor being. The term *evil*, therefore, can only signify a kind of absence of good and of being, for, since being, as such, is a good, the absence of the one necessarily involves the absence of the other."[13] Evil, as Calderón treats it in this *auto sacramental*, is pure negation within a substance, and the cause of evil paradoxically resides in a good. Only a being or a good can act or be a cause, and evil has no other cause than an accidental one. Aquinas believes that God wills that things in the natural order be good, but he is not the cause of evil. God is the cause, however, of the corruption and defects in all beings, but only because he wills the good in them. There is some good in every being, and the most evil of things still enriches some share of the perfection of the universe with its goodness.[14]

In *No hay más fortuna que Dios*, Mal, the negation of Bien, is sent into the world by the Devil, and is, ironically, a good which gives freedom to the characters of the *auto*, since they are free to follow this negation if they wish to do so. Freedom in a contingent creature like man, by the very fact of his contingency, is subject to erroneous judgment and can fail. It is only by misuse of freedom that man can do moral evil, since no matter what he does he will always be ontologically good. Natural law holds, however, that when man through his evil acts disturbs the pattern set for him, he ruins the resemblance which ought to exist between his acts and God's will. The ultimate reason that a human act is good is that it shares in the goodness of God, and the ultimate reason that an act is evil is that it goes contrary to his will in that it abuses the freedom given man.

Man may choose evil because of bad judgment on the part of his external and internal senses. Because he is primarily concerned with his material welfare, he may not recognize the fact that the moral good is intrinsically more desirable. In *No hay más fortuna que Dios*, the Devil believes that he has the advantage over la Justicia because of the weakness which is inherent in man's external senses, especially the vision:

> Mas la ventaja es mía,
> pues a los humanos ojos
> más cerca está el Mal que el Bien.
>
> JUSTICIA. A quien mirare ambicioso
> Bien y Mal, porque en la Esencia
> más lo está el Bien.
>
> (622)

All being is good, but the privation of goodness, evil, sometimes attracts man, especially through the sense most easily deceived, the sight. His senses can easily create an illusion as to what is beneficial to man.

Calderón returns to the theme of Original Sin, presenting el Bien and el Mal, who, in their desire to be the first to reach man, begin to fight.

> MAL.   Eso no;
> primero he de llegar yo;
> pues sabes que te prefiero
> desde el día que en pecado
> el Hombre nació; y así,
> el llegar primero a mí
> me toca.
>
> BIEN.   Si ya borrado
> con el Sacramento está
> del Bautismo ese delito,

y es Bien de Gracia Infinito
el que al hombre se le da,
primero es justo que el Bien
llegue, que no la actual
Culpa, de que eres el Mal
que hoy representas.

(622)

El Bien and el Mal drop their capes in a scuffle. La Malicia returns the capes, but gives that of el Mal to el Bien, and that of el Bien to el Mal. This is the cause of the confusion of the human characters, as they incorrectly interpret advantages or disadvantages in goods as they seek happiness. In the search for happiness man utilizes goods of fortune, goods of the body, goods of the soul, and all of these in conjunction. Calderón, in this *auto sacramental*, dramatizes man's utilization of these goods in his search for happiness and fulfillment in the natural order. Professor Parker says that Calderón "is not concerned to distinguish varying shades of good and evil in human actions, but is concentrating solely on the mistake made by the whole of weak and erring humanity—not only the mistake (in the supernatural order) of seeking for a happiness that is not God, but primarily the mistake (in the natural order) of failing to see where the excellence of nature really lies."[15] Not everything is good for man, and he must judge for himself what things are beneficial. Since human judgments are open to error he may mistake the apparent good for the true good. El Poder exemplifies this mistake in his failure to recognize the moral good; faced with good and evil, he does not discern carefully:

Ni a uno ni a otro conozco;
mas ¿qué me admiro, supuesto
que en la copia de criados
es del Poder argumento
tenerlos para mandarlos
y no para conocerlos?

(623)

He asks el Mal and el Bien if they know an object which will satisfy his every desire. This request may be interpreted as a search for the highest good, since it is a *divino objeto* which he seeks:

¿Cuál de vosotros, decidme,
sabrá de un divino objeto,
que en tantos aplausos, es
él solamente el empleo
más alto de mi Esperanza
y más digno de mi afecto,
según su Hermosura?

(623)

El Bien leads him to bookshelves where la Discreción is seated reading, suggesting that it is through the intellect that man is capable of knowing happiness. "Esta es la estancia, este el centro/ de la perfecta Hermosura,/ de quien yo avisarte debo" (623).

La Discreción, the cogitative sense, represents the gift of intelligence in man, which he ought to cultivate for good use. She is part of the natural reason of man which enables him to distinguish good from evil, so leading him to the perfect good. La Discreción defines herself as the center of all perfection:

Yo soy el Alma de todas
las Perfecciones, supuesto
que no hay virtud, que sin mí
logre su merecimiento,
pues no siendo virtud, soy
quien modera sus extremos
para que su elevación
subsista, siendo yo el medio.

(624)

She is the power that enables man not only to acquire knowledge but also to judge his own actions as harmful or beneficial to himself. Of course this power is not predetermined by nature; thus la Discreción, like the rest of the characters, errs in the beginning by attributing her status to fortune. According to her own definition, la Discreción stands at the center of moral perfection. She is the principle of moderation, and because she has the power to discern good and evil she can prevent virtue from becoming vice through excess and thus can lead man to happiness.

El Poder, after being led to the highest good that nature can offer him—*discreción*—acknowledges the worth of this intellectual power, but avoids the effort which would be required of him in gaining this good.

> No podrás negarme
> que para el glorioso efecto
> que me propones es fuerza
> que haya de pasar primero
> por molestias, por fatigas,
> vigilias, ansias y anhelos,
> que cuesta el estudio a quien
> ve el afán antes que el premio;
> no eres tú el Bien que yo busco.
> (624)

El Mal, dressed in the cape of el Bien, then leads el Poder to la Hermosura. El Poder falls prey to her immediately. It is not wrong to desire la Hermosura, since her natural gifts are good; what is wrong is that he desires her to excess—without *discreción*. His desire for natural beauty, untempered by moderation, leads him to adore her as a false deity. La Hermosura is complacent in her vainglory, and all of the characters come and pay homage to her. They are all trying to find happiness, and they attribute partial fulfillment of this desire to her. After she is praised by all of the characters, Calderón presents a moral warning in the form of two choruses singing at the same time, continuing the confusion in the minds of the characters:

> CORO 1.°   Alábese la Hermosura
>   de que si en algún concepto
>   el hombre es pequeño mundo,
>   la Mujer pequeño cielo.
>   . . . .
> CORO 2.°   No la Hermosura se alabe,
>   pues de dos veces muriendo,
>   una, con el Dueño yace
>   y otra, yace sin el Dueño.
>   (626)

This is the confusion which besets man: ontological beauty leads him to delude himself in his choice of goods. The characters of the *auto*, in their confused state, decide to enjoy the beauty of worldly goods without discretion. The error they commit is "de hacer diosa a la Fortuna,/ y no a la Justicia" (628). Ignorance is the root of this mistake. They neither understand from whence the goods come, nor can they comprehend the nature of these goods. They do not make an intellectual effort to clarify the mystery, as they feel satisfied with the natural goods which they now possess. El Pobre's statement is typical of the sentiments of all:

> Ni entiendo lo que me dices
> ni solicito entenderlo,
> cuando me trae la Fortuna
> a mendigar el sustento.
>
> BIEN. Si pensaras que no es
> la Fortuna quien lo ha hecho,
> sino Dios, tú me entendieras.
>
> POBRE. Vete y no me des consejos,
> pues que no me das limosnas.
>
> (629)

The object of man's happiness must lie in something below him, in man himself, or in something above him. The finite goods below man with which he can surround himself in this world—power, honor, fame, comfort, and riches—can be possessed with unhappiness. Because of the hardships they impose and because of their uneven distribution, these are called goods of fortune. Some receive these goods without labor (el Poder and la Hermosura), while others cannot obtain them even with great effort (el Pobre and la Labranza). These temporal goods can create a state of unhappiness because they are owned with anxiety and must be left behind at death. The thesis of natural law is that the goods of fortune are intended to be means, not ends in themselves. They are to be utilized by man, not man by them. In the *auto*, Death, in the form of a skeleton, comes to take away the two capes and the goods that have dropped from the Tree of Good and Evil, exclaiming:

Humo, polvo, nada y viento.
. . . .
Sacar de donde cae una
Hermosura, un Esqueleto,
en cuyas manos miráis
que van a dar, como a centro,
desde el báculo al bastón
y desde la azada al cetro;
y, pues el espejo suyo
a todos sirve de espejo,
temed, mortales, temed,
que entre el Bien y el Mal es cierto
no hay más fortuna que Dios.
(631)

Death thus reveals to the characters that the goods of fortune are not the purpose for which man lives. These words shatter their confidence, as they fear the emptiness which now awaits them. All are left unfulfilled in their desire for happiness. The goods of fortune have disappeared, leaving them with the physical and spiritual goods which they themselves possess. According to Aquinas neither the goods of the body—strength, beauty, and the like—nor the goods of the soul—knowledge, virtue—taken separately, can make men happy, since the body cannot satisfy the soul, nor can the soul satisfy the body. No matter how much man may possess of the goods of fortune or the goods of body and soul, he will not be satisfied with them. Since he is satisfied neither with temporal material goods nor with those which are a part of him, and since none of these things taken separately or combined make him completely happy, there must be something above man which will bring about his complete satisfaction. His intellect desires to know all truth and his will desires perfect goodness. By the process of elimination, then, as the characters of *No hay más fortuna que Dios* discover, happiness is to be sought in the only object which can fulfill man's desires—God; no lesser being will suffice.

The characters in this *auto sacramental* are summoned to believe in and trust in God and his distributive justice. Acceptance of the burdens that accompany la Cruz will not destroy but will enhance natural happiness by lessening the suffering in life and making these burdens bearable. La Justicia explains the administering of justice by telling man that God is the first cause.[16] *No hay más fortuna que Dios* follows the tenets of natural law by showing that man, through natural reason and experience, is capable of knowing that there exists an order of efficient cause and effect in the world, that certain beings cause others to exist. It is not conceivable that a finite being with its limitations should be the cause of itself, since it would have first to exist in order to cause itself to exist. It needs another cause. Calderón follows Aquinas's view that there must be a first efficient cause, since there cannot be a series of subordinate efficient causes. God is the first efficient cause of distributive justice. La Justicia explains to the characters:

> Dios, primer Causa de todo,
> es quien llega a repartir
> el Bien que no conocéis
> y el Mal que no distinguís.
>
> . . . .
> Vive en tu suerte contento
> (¡oh mortal!), y al discurrir
> que al fin se canta la Gloria,
> busca la Gloria en el fin.
>
> (633)

In his theory of eternal law Thomas holds that God, as the first cause, directs all creatures to their ends. He has willed not only the law but the means for man to obey this law.[17] Natural law, the eternal law applied to creatures, is the uniform inclination that beings have to attain their definite ends. Man, through his natural reason, ought to seek his ultimate goal in the possession of God. As the characters of *No hay más fortuna que Dios* learn, it is only through acceptance of God's providence and proper use of goods that man can find happiness. All things are subject to divine providence as they partake of the eternal law, but man is subject to divine providence in a more perfect way, since he partakes of a share of providence through use of his free will.[18]

Natural law decrees that since God wills that all creatures attain their ends, he also wills the means necessary to fulfill those ends. The means which man uses are the goods of body and soul. These goods are powerful enough to produce the effect desired which is that man act for an end. They are also suited to man's rational and free nature, since he can first choose the goods and then choose the way in which he utilizes them. Through human conduct he ought to aim for the highest good and the last end, which alone will satisfy his desires and make him happy. It is in this respect that the characters in the *auto* fail to attain human fulfillment; they choose to follow la Fortuna, rejecting la Cruz until the end of the play. In the final scene the Eucharist appears and la Justicia explains God's plan:

> Por inmensos
> Sacramentos, de quien es
> este de la Gracia aumento.
> Y así, como principal
> de todos los Sacramentos,
> le administra la Justicia,
> triste al malo, alegre al bueno,
> para que a vista del Bien
> y al Mal le adoréis diciendo.
> *(Canta.)*
> Ama a un Dios que te ama,
> que hermosa y gentil
> no es deidad la fortuna, no, no,
> la Justicia, sí.
> (633)

In this *auto sacramental* Calderón dramatizes the idea that through natural reason man can come to know that God is the first cause of the good and of the end, and that the only way he can find happiness is in the possession of the highest good, which is God, since *no hay más fortuna que Dios.*

Chapter Seven

A Dios por razón de estado

Ángel Valbuena Prat classifies *El gran teatro del mundo, No hay más fortuna que Dios*, and *A Dios por razón de estado* as *autos filosóficos y teológicos*, in which Calderón synthesizes philosophical and theological doctrines.[1] *No hay más fortuna que Dios* is the most philosophical in content of the three, while *A Dios por razón de estado* emphasizes biblical narrative. The theological material of *A Dios por razón de estado*, drawn from the Acts of the Apostles, serves as the framework of the play, while the philosophical content, man's search for God through use of natural reason, is represented by the dramatic action. In this *auto sacramental* Calderón dramatizes an ethical problem related to natural law—man's knowledge of God as the first cause by use of natural reason complemented by divine revelation obliges him to acknowledge and worship God. In his examination of the philosophical content of this *auto*, Ludwig Pfandl observes that Calderón follows Thomistic doctrine in that natural reason is able to know metaphysical order:

Calderón, en su auto sacramental *A Dios por razón de Estado*, hace que Dionisio Areopagita, que representa la razón, después de haber luchado largo tiempo en vano por alcanzar la verdad, sea convertido por el discurso de San Pablo sobre el dios desconocido, símbolo del racionalismo cristiano. En esta lucha del alma reflexiva, glorifica Calderón la manera de ser de la neoescolástica española, ya que en el fondo no es ella otra cosa que la vivificación, la crítica y la penetración de la doctrina de Santo Tomás, el cual había interpretado racionalmente el "credo ut intelligam" agustiniano en esta forma: creo para penetrar reflexivamente en el contenido de la fe.[2]

According to Thomas Aquinas, man was created with the intellectual faculties necessary to observe the natural law and to explore the mysteries of the universe. Noting the motion, order, harmony, and design in the universe, man comes to have knowledge of God as the first cause. From this knowledge of God's existence comes man's obligation to worship him.

The *sermón representable* of this *auto sacramental* draws its material from the Acts of the Apostles, using in particular the accounts of two conversions, the Apostle Paul's and Dionysius's. As the *auto* begins el Ingenio declares that he and el Pensamiento will search for God:

> Trascendiendo
> (supuesto que no se da
> en lo alegórico tiempo
> ni lugar) todos los ritos,
> hasta que halle ley en ellos
> de un Dios que, ignoto y pasible,
> le cuadre a mi entendimiento.
> (857)

El Ingenio, representing Dionysius of Areopagus, is the central character of the *auto* and takes part in the dramatic action from beginning to end. Dionysius's conversion, which is so closely related to the action of *A Dios por razón de estado*, takes place, according to the biblical account (Acts 17:34), after Paul's sermon at the Areopagus. Through the personified figures of el Pensamiento and el Ingenio, Calderón analyzes the moral conflicts in the search for God and presents the concepts necessary to form the Pauline arguments for God's existence and purpose.

Calderón follows Aquinas in his treatment of natural reason. El Pensamiento and el Ingenio complement one another, as the former says:[3]

> De mi parte te ofrezco
> asistirte hasta que apures
> de sacrificio tan nuevo
> la causa, pues a los dos
> en alcance del misterio
> a mí me toca el pensarlo
> y a ti te toca el saberlo.
> (851)

El Pensamiento represents qualities of the imagination and the cogitative sense which Aquinas treats in his analysis of the internal senses.[4] For Thomas the imagination retains images of past external sense experience and creates sensory images from this past experience. Although this faculty is an essential and valuable part of natural reason, the intellect must operate with a controlled imagination, as Calderón demonstrates in the opening scene of this play. The cogitative sense (*vis cogitativa*) is the estimative power, the function of which is to know what is beneficial and what harmful in the sensible order. El Ingenio exhibits properties of the central sense and the memory. The central sense, the link between the external world and man's consciousness, perceives the objects of the external senses and their activities. Its function is to correlate the various objects of the external senses and to make man aware of his act of sensation. The faculty *memoria* recalls past experiences as favorable or unfavorable, perfecting the imagination by placing images in their proper setting and time. *Reminiscientia*, part of *memoria*, is the power of recall which operates in conjunction with reason to employ a type of syllogistic process. Thus together el Pensamiento and el Ingenio represent a composite of natural reason in the scholastic sense, and as such they direct the external as well as the internal sense powers in man's search for truth.

Calderón relates the apostolic career of Paul to the wanderings of el Pensamiento and el Ingenio through Europe and Asia, Athens being their starting point. The apostolate of Athens was an extraordinary challenge for Paul. This was the first time that he had faced such a highly critical audience—speculation, argument, and discussion being a daily part of their intellectual life. It was there that he delivered his famous speech before the Areopagus. Although Paul's preaching met with almost complete failure, the Athenians did not persecute him for his beliefs. Paul began his visit in his usual manner, arguing with the Jews in the synagogue and strolling in the marketplace in the style of Socrates, explaining his beliefs to the common people. Epicureans and Stoics, members of the two most important philosophical schools of the time, met with the apostle and brought him to the Areopagus, where the judicial court met to pass on the competence of new religious lecturers.

Paul's speech, a challenge to pagan philosophy, met with some success. Instead of the references to holy scripture which he used with the Jews, he employed natural theology, a doctrine held by the pagan poets, to explain God's creation. Calderón uses the first part of Paul's speech in the discussion that el Pensamiento and el Ingenio have with la Gentilidad about the inscription *Ignoto Deo* which is found on the frontispiece of a temple. The apostle began his sermon at the Areopagus by praising his audience's religiosity, referring to the inscription that he had chanced to see on an Athenian altar:

Men of Athens, I perceive that in every way you are very religious. For as I passed along, and observed the objects of your worship, I found also an altar with this inscription, "To an unknown god." What therefore you worship as unknown, this I proclaim to you. The God who made the world and everything in it, being Lord of heaven and earth, does not live in shrines made by man, nor is he served by human hands, as though he needed anything, since he himself gives to all men life and breath and everything. And he made from one every nation of men to live on all the face of the earth, having determined allotted periods and the boundaries of their habitation, that they should seek God, in the hope that they might feel after him and find him. (Acts 17:22-27)

Paul stressed the idea of God as the Creator and the Preserver of the universe and mankind. He showed his intellectual skill by pointing out the ideas which the gospel had in common with Stoicism, using the verse from a stoic poet, Aratus of Soli, "For we are indeed his offspring," to challenge the belief in pantheism and the practice of idolatry:

Yet he is not far from each one of us, for "In him we live and move and have our being"; as even some of your poets have said, "For we are indeed his offspring." Being then God's offspring, we ought not to think that the Deity is like gold, or silver, or stone, a representation by the art and imagination of man. The times of ignorance God overlooked, but now he commands all men everywhere to repent, because he has fixed a day on which he will judge the world in righteousness by a man whom he has appointed, and of this he has given assurance to all men by raising him from the dead. (Acts 17:27-31)

"The times of ignorance" were past as far as Paul was concerned, and men ought to repent because the world was going to be judged. The apostle's mention of the resurrection of the dead divided his audiences; while some scoffed, others converted, among them Dionysius the Areopagite. It is this conversion and that of Paul himself that Calderón uses as the structure of his *auto sacramental*. In *A Dios por razón de estado* God is revealed in nature to the pagan, in natural theology to the Athenians, and in scriptures and arguments to the Jews and the Moslems.

In the opening scene of the *auto* el Ingenio succeeds in subduing el Pensamiento who, *vestido de loco*, represents unrestrained imagination. They both hear music and voices singing:

> "Gran Dios que ignoramos,
> abrevia el tiempo
> y haz que te conozcamos,
> pues te creemos."
>
> (850)

In their attempt to fathom the problem inherent in these words they discover a mountain on which there is an open temple, the Areopagus, with an inscription on the frontispiece—*Ignoto Deo*. The inscription on the temple and the song coming from within, *Gran Dios que ignoramos*, imply natural religion, a knowledge of God through natural reason, as el Ingenio indicates in a syllogistic argument:

> Y es tan cierto,
> que a no ser comunicable
> Dios, no fuera Dios: lo pruebo
> con que imperfecto el bien fuera
> no comunicado: luego
> no pudiendo el ser de Dios
> ser nunca bien imperfecto,
> ha de ser comunicado:
> . . . .
>   Escuchemos
> qué género de hostia dan
> al Dios ignorado estos
> que, ignorándole, le aclaman,
> y ya alumbrados y ciegos,
> de su templo a los umbrales,
> dicen cantando y tañendo.
>
> (851)

Calderón follows natural law, implying that man, a finite being, is not
able to understand an infinite being completely, while God as a
perfect being communicates with all mankind, even those who are
ignorant of him.

According to natural law, worship ought to follow man's knowledge of God. Aquinas believes that natural religion comprises only
the duties to God which man is able to discover through human
reason unaided by revelation, while supernatural religion depends on
some revelation by God.[5]

The starting point of natural religion, the obligation of worship
resulting from knowledge of God's existence, is encountered when el
Pensamiento and el Ingenio hear the song which represents the
religion of la Gentilidad.

> MUJER 1.ª (*Cant.*) Dios no sabido hasta ahora,
> pues solamente por fe
> la Gentilidad te cree,
> entre los dioses que adora;
> permite que quien te ignora
> te conozca, a cuyo efecto:
> (*Bailando cruzados atrave-
> sados. Música.*)
> "Gran Dios que ignoramos,
> abrevia el tiempo."
> MUJER 2.ª Ser que solo imaginado
> te adivina la noticia,
> tal vez Dios de la justicia
> y tal vez Dios del agrado;
> permite que declarado
> te merezca el amor nuestro.
>
> (852)

The contradiction inherent in the religion of la Gentilidad is the first
intellectual problem that el Ingenio and el Pensamiento face. After
observing the rites of la Gentilidad, el Ingenio poses the first question
about this religion:

> ¿Cómo es posible que haya
> en la ignorancia pretexto
> que a eso os persuada?
>
> (852)

Natural law decrees that man is dependent on God and that his act of worship is due to God, arising out of knowledge of his existence. La Gentilidad, surprised at the question of el Ingenio, wants to know the identity of this intruder. El Ingenio replies in a soliloquy:

> Amante soy de las ciencias,
> por cuyo rendido afecto,
> siendo Philos el Amor,
> y Sophia la Ciencia, puedo
> decir que Philosophía
> es la dama que más quiero.
>
> (852)

El Ingenio identifies himself with Paul's disciple Dionysius the Areopagite, who used philosophical doctrines to build a mystical Christian theology. Dionysius believed that all things refer back to God either as the principle or as the end. God possesses all the perfections of his creatures, but in his transcendence he is sometimes obscure. As the principle of all things and the finality of everything, God attracts all beings to himself.

The allegorical role of Dionysius the philosopher is the part which el Ingenio plays in this particular *auto:*

> Es mi nombre o ha de serlo
> en la nueva alegoría
> del acto que represento,
> yendo de historial sentido
> y alegórico compuesto,
> Dionisio, que significa
> lo acendrado y lo supremo
> de aquella divinidad
> del alma, como diciendo
> que es quinta esencia del alma
> el nombre de que me precio.
>
> (852)

El Ingenio and el Pensamiento together represent the intellect which progresses towards truth through reasoning, the natural movement of discursive intelligence. They represent natural reason, which, according to natural-law philosophy, is independent of faith.

La Gentilidad explains what she represents and describes her religious ceremony to el Pensamiento and el Ingenio:

> Yo soy la Gentilidad...
>
> . . . .
>
> al ceremonioso rito
> de los devotos festejos
> de un ignoto Dios, a cuya
> causa ves sin ara el templo,
> altar ni estatua, porque
> aunque noticia tenemos
> dél, es noticia remota.
>
> (853)

Calderón thus emphasizes the idea that there is a natural inclination to worship God imbedded in la Gentilidad. God is knowable in the natural order, although remotely, and obligation to worship stems from this knowledge. As la Gentilidad states, Stoicism was investigating

> la sacra naturaleza
> de los Dioses, discurriendo
> en una primera causa,
> a cuyo cargo quisieron
> que estuviese reducido
> el orden del Universo;
> destos, pues, al creer que todo
> debajo está de un gobierno.
>
> (853)

The Stoics held that the universe was animated by the divine Logos who unified the diverse beings into a harmonious hierarchy. They conceived of God as the universal soul, a theory related to certain of Plato's teachings.

> Y desde el mayor lucero
> a la menor planta, dijo
> uno había un Dios Supremo,
> toda manos, toda ojos,
> toda oídos, a que luego
> causa añadió de las causas.
>
> (853)

God, as the cause of causes, was the divine reason in the order and beauty of the world. Man attained happiness, according to the Stoics, by leading a life which coincided with this divine reason, thus obeying the laws of nature and his own conscience. After hearing the explanation of stoic philosophy by la Gentilidad, el Ingenio neither approves nor disapproves; he wants to investigate this way of life further before he makes a decision about its moral worth. El Ingenio and el Pensamiento then observe a *máscara* which represents the second of Aquinas's metaphysical demonstrations of the existence of God.

> MUSICA.   "Al sacrificio del Dios Ignorado
> acude devoto y festivo el afecto."
> (*vueltas en cruz*.)
> UNA VOZ.   "Mostrando si es causa de todas las causas,
> que humano responda a la causa el efecto."
> (854)

Thomas's second demonstration of God begins with a fact of experience, that man observes in the world an order of efficient cause and effect. Certain beings cause others to exist.

The second way is from the nature of the efficient cause. In the world of sense we find there is an order of efficient causes. There is no case known (neither is it, indeed, possible) in which a thing is found to be the efficient cause of itself; for so it would be prior to itself, which is impossible. Now in efficient causes it is not possible to go on to infinity, because in all efficient causes following in order, the first is the cause of the intermediate cause, and the intermediate is the cause of the ultimate cause, whether the intermediate cause be several, or one only. Now to take away the cause is to take away the effect. Therefore, if there be no first cause among efficient causes, there will be no ultimate, nor any intermediate cause. But if in efficient causes it is possible to go on to infinity, there will be no first efficient cause, neither will there be an ultimate effect, nor any intermediate efficient causes; all of which is plainly false. Therefore it is necessary to admit a first efficient cause, to which everyone gives the name of God.[6]

According to Aquinas it is inconceivable that a limited being be its own efficient cause, because it would first have to exist in order to cause itself to exist.

While el Pensamiento and el Ingenio ponder the ideas represented in the *máscara* there is an earthquake and an eclipse. The characters become confused. La Gentilidad asks el Ingenio to explain the cause of the phenomena. The latter responds, "Que expira el cielo o su Hacedor padece" (855). This puzzles la Gentilidad greatly, and she asks el Ingenio a series of questions related to scholastic philosophy:

> ¿Quien dice Hacedor no dice
> primer principio?
>
> . . . .
> ¿Quien dice primer principio
> no dice poder inmenso,
> de quien se origina todo
> antes y después eterno?
>
> . . . .
>   ¿Pues cómo,
> si solo un Dios puede serlo,
> ha de padecer? ¿No implica
> Dios y pasible?
>
>   (855)

El Ingenio admits that the first two questions are answered in the affirmative. In response to the third he tells la Gentilidad that her own argument answers her inquiries and that he must search further for the truth:

> INGENIO. Si Dios ignorado implica,
>   y tú crees que puede haberlo,
>   ¿qué mucho que dude yo
>   que haya, el ejemplar siguiendo,
>   Dios y pasible? Y así,
>   entre tu yerro y mi yerro,
>   tú creyendo y yo dudando,
>   a discurrir me resuelvo.
>
>   (855)

El Ingenio does not believe the argument set forth by la Gentilidad, nor does he believe that he himself has the correct answers to the puzzling questions. For this reason he and el Pensamiento will continue their search:

INGENIO.
 Discurriendo
el mundo por cuantas leyes,
cuantos ritos, cuantos fueros
una y otra religión
tienen, hasta que mi anhelo,
haciendo razón de Estado
la que ahora de dudar tengo,
la causa halle de las causas
que tenga (toda oídos siendo,
toda ojos, toda manos)
la conveniencia de serlo
para padecer.

(856)

La Gentilidad can proceed no further in the intellectual pursuit on which natural reason will embark. Believing that she has the answer, she no longer searches for truth; for her there cannot be a God who is *pasible* and the cause of causes at the same time. El Ingenio concedes that the phenomena of sky and earth which have occurred present a mystery for which he lacks an answer, but as natural reason he will attempt to find this answer:

Puede algún misterio haber,
que por ahora no comprendo;
pero en lo pecaminoso
no es posible haber misterio
que a la razón natural
no repugne.

(856)

El Ingenio and el Pensamiento next encounter el Ateísmo, of whom they ask the cause of the earthquake and the eclipse. He offers them an explanation which compares the four elements of the earth to the four humors of the body; as the body is subject to sickness so is the earth subject to the phenomena that the characters have experienced. El Ateísmo does not care to waste his time and effort searching for the first cause of the earthquake and eclipse:

Nunca en eso me cansara
yo, porque nunca creyera
que le hallara ing ni pudiera.

(858)

In answer to the questions el Ingenio asks about the cause of man, his soul, his being, and the harmony of the universe, el Ateísmo answers that all he knows is that he was born, but he does not know why. Concerning the question of the creation of man he says, "Puedo pensar que la prima/ materia se corrompió/ y al primer hombre engendró" (858). He does not believe that the soul is immortal, and he does not care about a cause of causes. The only thing which he knows is that there is birth and death in the world. He wishes to discuss the matter no further. El Pensamiento adds comic relief to this serious scene by losing control of himself for a moment:

> Amigo, si no hay primera
> causa, ¿quién nueve mi acción
> a darte este mojicón?
> (858)

El Ateísmo flees from el Pensamiento and el Ingenio calms his companion so that natural reason may continue its search for truth. They have not found a satisfactory answer to their questions in the many gods of la Gentilidad, nor are they satisfied with the opinions of el Ateísmo, who believes in no god. They wish to meet somebody who believes in one God. This desire is fulfilled as they meet Africa, in Moorish costume, celebrating the earthquake and the eclipse since she believes them to be signs that the Prophet is coming.

> Aquel Profeta, que yo
> previne en sus luces bellas,
> diciendo este eclipse en ellas,
> que presto a vernos vendrá.
> (859)

In response to the inquiries of el Ingenio, Africa tells him that she believes in one God, as do the Jews:

> Su Dios espera el hebreo,
> de quien los principios tomo
> para mi ley, aunque inquieta
> la esperanza de los dos,
> dicta que él aguarda a un Dios
> y yo aguardo su profeta.
> (860)

El Ingenio sees a contradiction in the religion of Africa in that it contains two conflicting laws:

> ¿Pues cómo puede en dos
> leyes servirse? Ve aquí,
> que una ley me da un precepto
> y que la otra ley no la acepta.
> ¿Es justo que me prometa
> de dos causas un efecto?
>   (860)

Africa accepts the precepts given to her by the Koran and does not care whether there is a single law or not. She invites el Ingenio to witness a ritual in which each man dances with various women. This brings up the question of polygamy, which is contrary to natural law, and el Ingenio asks her:

> Si es contrato natural
> amor que confirma el trato,
> ¿cómo puede ser contrato
> lícito el que no es igual?
>   (861)

Marriage was considered both by Aristotle and by Aquinas to be a natural institution. Aristotle argues that man and woman form couples by nature and that their functions in life are divided from the start. Children are the bond of union between the sexes, since children are the good common to both man and woman and that which is common holds them together.[7] Aquinas presents a more formal argument for marriage as a natural institution, using as his basis Aristotle's statements.[8] According to Aquinas, it is evident that natural law intends the continuance of the human race and that the care of the child is charged to the parents since they are the cause of its existence. Nature therefore demands a relatively permanent union between the sexes, guaranteed by contract. The primary end of marriage is the rearing of children, while the secondary end is the satisfaction of the human desire for sexual pleasure, love, and companionship. Polygamy goes counter to natural law in that the father cannot train the children of many wives as he could if they were of one wife. The love and companionship that exist between husband

and wife are weakened by being single in one direction and divided in the other. El Ingenio and el Pensamiento decide to leave Africa since she cannot answer their questions about God, and since they feel that her marriage arrangement is basically unnatural. El Ingenio tells Africa that the God for whom he is searching must be an entity:

> De sí solo, en sí y por sí,
> incomprensible y divino,
> y siendo tal, cierto es que
> dará su fe verdadera
> a quien quiera, y como quiera
> y cuando quiera, sin que
> este se pueda quejar
> de que al otro se la dio,
> puesto que a todos dotó
> de razón para buscar
> la mejor.
>
> (861)

Africa scorns el Ingenio as a stupid philosopher and continues to dance and sing as she awaits her prophet.

Since el Ingenio and el Pensamiento have not found the answers for which they are searching in la Gentilidad with many gods, in el Ateísmo with no god, or in Africa with one god and no law, they now decide to look for a religion which has one God and one law. Calderón returns to the biblical narrative as la Sinagoga appears, representing such a religion. She is accompanied by Paul, whom el Ingenio recognizes:

> ¿No es Pablo con quien viene,
> de quien me hizo amigo fiel
> la escuela de Gamaliel
> por el ingenio que tiene?
>
> (861)

La Sinagoga gives Paul a decree and sends him to Damascus, in a scene following the biblical account of Paul's conversion.[9] While Paul is in Damascus el Ingenio and la Sinagoga discuss the cause and significance of the earthquake and the eclipse. La Sinagoga rejects the idea that el Autor has anything to do with these phenomena.

No ha sido, no ha sido,
si ya no quieres que sea
autor suyo un sedicioso
nazareno, escandaloso,
que en Palestina y Judea,
en Samaria y Galilea,
predicando aquestos días
dio a entender que era el Mesías,
Hijo de Dios verdadero
que ha tantos siglos que espero.
(862-63)

She then relates to el Ingenio the history of the Jews and their religion, telling him that she believes in one God. She explains that the written law in the form of the Ten Commandments complements the natural law:

Si entre tantos beneficios
fue el mayor darme su ley
el mármol escrita, siendo
su mismo dedo el cincel,
por quien la ley natural
vino a elevar y crecer
su primer candor, subiendo
de dos preceptos a diez.
(863)

The two *preceptos* of la Sinagoga are: do good and avoid evil, and do unto others as you would have them do unto you. She considers the Ten Commandments to be derived from natural law. According to Thomistic theory, God's direct intervention and revelation impose divine positive law on man; such is the case with the Ten Commandments. Although it is true that these Commandments are inferences from natural law, they differ from it, not in content, but in mode of promulgation. Since the Commandments were promulgated by external signs, they are considered to be divine positive law. The first and main reason for divine revelation is to aid man in attaining his last end;[10] another reason is that man's judgment is uncertain in following and making laws. In order that man may know which one to follow, God has given him divine help through his law. Human law in itself is not sufficient to lead man to his last end, since it cannot punish or forbid all evil acts. Because of his supernatural end, man is directed in a more perfect way by divine law and its perfect sanction.

Thus in *A Dios por razón de estado*, la Sinagoga with her Ten Commandments comes closer to the Thomistic view of God's nature than any of the other characters, with the exception of Paul, who experiences a miracle which reveals more to him than is known to the other characters. She cannot comprehend, however, that the Son of God should come at this time; according to her calculations it is not yet time. Neither can she understand why God would kill his Son, nor why the Son could suffer or die, since he is supposed to have a divine nature. Similarly, el Ingenio and el Pensamiento are confused by some of the beliefs of la Sinagoga:

> INGENIO.　Que si adora (como dijo)
> sólo un Dios, ¿cómo despúés
> dijo que a su Hijo esperaba?
> ¿Hijo y Padre fuerza no es
> que sean dos? Pues ¿cómo a uno
> adora solo?
>
> (864)

Only divine revelation can answer these questions. For this Calderón returns to Paul's vision in the biblical text:

> VOZ.　　Pablo.
> (*Suena dentro un trueno y
> vese como una luz de un relám-
> pago.*)
>
> .　.　.　.　.
> 　　¿Por qué
> me persigues?
>
> .　.　.　.　.
> PABLO.　El rayo, Señor, detén,
> basta el trueno de tu voz.
>
> (864)

Paul falls from his horse and loses his sight. After accusing la Sinagoga of treachery for her part in the death of Christ, Paul explains the doctrine of the Trinity as best he can:

Una en los tres la deidad,
uno en los tres el poder,
uno en los tres el amor
y uno en los tres el saber,
cierto que en la esencia es uno,
siendo en las personas tres.

(865)

Up to this point natural reason (el Pensamiento and el Ingenio) is satisfied with Paul's statements. The apostle then explains the purpose of the Trinity as a means for man as a finite being to be forgiven for his infinite sin against God. Both natural reason and la Sinagoga are satisfied with this and with Paul's mention of Mary; but when he tells them that Christ the Messiah has arrived, la Sinagoga objects strongly. In the stichomythic conversation that follows, Paul answers all of the objections of la Sinagoga referring to the fulfillment of the prophecies of the Old Testament. El Ingenio then calls la Gentilidad who represents Europe, la Sinagoga (Asia), Africa and el Ateísmo (America) before him and tells them that he has received the answer to all of his questions from Paul. Although not everything that the apostle has said is understood completely, natural reason has accepted the message of Paul. In order that the mystery of the Trinity may be explained fully, three laws are introduced to man. La Ley Natural appears at the foot of a tree which has a serpent wrapped around it and addresses herself to la Gentilidad, making known her principles:

Que amase a Dios más que a mí,
y a mi prójimo después
como a mí.

(867)

La Ley Escrita comes on stage next and dictates the Ten Commandments to the characters, and lastly la Ley de Gracia, with a cross in her hand and her eyes bound (*vendados los ojos, como pintan la Fe*) enters and introduces the seven sacraments which flow from the *Fuente de la Gracia:*

Por Ley de Gracia soy
la superior a las tres.

> No solo esos diez preceptos
> confirmó en mí; mas porque
> su cumplimiento tuviese
> fianza a no fallecer,
> los fortaleció de siete
> sacramentos, que allí ves
> de la Fuente de la Gracia
> perennemente correr.
>
> (868)

Finally, with the help of la Ley de Gracia and the seven sacraments, el Ingenio comprehends all that Paul has told him. Resuming the role of Dionysius, he accepts Paul's religion:

> Llegando a amar y creer
> por razón de Estado cuando
> faltara la de la fe.
>
> (868)

Thus, following the precepts of natural law, Calderón demonstrates that natural reason can come to know, love, and believe in God *por razón de estado* if not by faith. With the statement *por razón de estado*, Calderón refers to Aquinas's fifth demonstration of God which has to do with the governance of things.

> The fifth way is taken from the governance of the world. We see that things which lack intelligence, such as natural bodies, act for an end, and this is evident from their acting always, or nearly always, in the same way, so as to obtain the best result. Hence it is plain that not fortuitously, but designedly, do they achieve their end. Now whatever lacks intelligence cannot move towards an end, unless it be directed by some being endowed with knowledge and intelligence; as the arrow is shot to its mark by the archer. Therefore some intelligent being exists by whom all natural things are directed to their end; and this being we call God.[11]

Calderón demonstrates that man can know God through natural reason's observance of the governance of things—the natural law. This knowledge is then perfected by written law and faith. Once man is convinced of the truth of religion he is morally bound to accept it, just as, if he were convinced it was false, he would be obliged to reject it. If he is doubtful he naturally ought to withhold judgment until he is convinced one way or another.

In *A Dios por razón de estado*, Calderón has combined a presentation of these three states of mind—acceptance, rejection, and suspension of judgment—with biblical themes and scholastic philosophy. In the biblical framework of the conversions of Paul and Dionysius, Calderón presents natural reason's intellectual progress toward knowledge of God. The metaphysical theories of Aquinas pertaining to the knowledge of God stand between those of Augustine, which emphasize the role of intuition, and the agnostic views of the Averroists and the followers of Maimonides. *A Dios por razón de estado* follows the tenets of Aquinas's natural law in showing that God is knowable through natural reason's observance of the motion, order, and design of the universe. La Ley Natural, la Ley Escrita, and la Ley de Gracia aid in this process of acquiring knowledge which is dramatized through the allegorical characters of Paul and Dionysius. The obligation to worship God follows as a conclusion:

> Por razón de Estado cuando
> faltara la de la fe.
> (869)

Chapter Eight

Conclusion

The dramatic use of the precepts of natural-law ethics accurately reflects the social morality and the literary theories of drama prevalent in the Golden Age. The dramatic critics of this era, interpreting the poetics of Aristotle and Horace, thought that art should instruct and delight. For them imitation was, as Aristotle implied, natural to man and a source of pleasure. When moral doctrine was used as an object of imitation, both ends of art, *enseñar* and *deleitar*, were fulfilled. Bances Candamo has this in mind when he speaks of the moral obligations of dramatists:

Quien diuierte al Rudo pueblo tiene dos obligaciones; la primera, que es de diuertirle inculpablemente, es indispensable en el que escriue; la segunda, que es de diuertirle aprouechándole, es mui combeniente y mui conforme a su instituto . . . Horacio quiere que se mezcle lo vtil con lo dulce y, finalmente, donde trataremos de la Poesía se verá quánta sea su obligación a no contentarse un tan gran arte con sola la vana delectación del sonido. Esta precissión es maior en los Poetas cómicos assí por ser más limado y censurado su estudio, como por ser para el vulgo, que por la maior parte ni vee otras historias, ni saue otros exemplares de la vida que los que le expone la comedia, y suele oi encontrar vnos Maestros, a quien su rusticidad da la lei y el arte pues haciendo venales sus obras sólo atienden en ellas al gusto de el Pueblo y a la vtilidad de las farsas, sin lleuar otro fin en su trabajo. ¿Qué errores no cometerá quien va sólo a agradar a hombres cuio gusto se manda por la causalidad de su antojo y no por la discreción de su razón?[1]

According to Spanish theorists, moral philosophy in drama not only appealed to man's rational nature and his love for learning, it fulfilled both the utilitarian function and the aesthetic purpose of drama.

Of course the intellectual climate of a period in history has a great deal to do with the ideas that appear in drama.[2] As the theater of

the twentieth century has been influenced by Freud and existen-
tialism, so the drama of the Golden Age was influenced by neopla-
tonism and natural-law philosophy. The dramatists contributed largely
to the climate of opinion of sixteenth- and seventeenth-century Spain
for they not only reflected the ideas of this era but also helped to
form them. The precepts of natural-law ethics formed an intrinsic part of
the theater of the Golden Age, but the combination of philosophy and
drama was hardly unique to this period. As Eric Bentley said: "Drama,
at its birth, is an intellectual thing. Western intellect is a Greek inven-
tion, and the Greeks put it to use not in philosophy only but in drama.
The two were not then so far apart. Even for Socrates philosophy
was not only dialectics, it was also spoken dialogue: it would seem
that he never wrote down a word. In teaching the West to speak,
Greece invited the West to believe that the spoken word is the proper
vehicle of mind and spirit.[3]

It was general practice in Counter-Reformation Spain to use
philosophy for moral and religious purposes. The resurgence of
scholastic philosophy, especially Thomistic natural-law ethics, and its
combination with literature came as a reaction to the Reformation.
Drama usually seeks and reflects great intellectual battles. In the case
of sixteenth- and seventeenth-century Spain the great battle was for
the survival of her orthodoxy.

The drama did not elaborate ideas as did the novels and historical
treatises of this period; instead, it presented both intellectually and
emotionally a concentrated interaction of concepts.[4] Golden Age
dramatists relied on theology in their works which were medieval in
some aspects, but their plays were much richer in their dramatic
effect than the medieval cycles. Some of the dramas, especially the
autos sacramentales, were doctrinal in content, didactic in intention,
and part of an unbroken tradition of the Middle Ages.[5]

The philosophy and theology which appear in Golden Age drama
reflect the social morality of this epoch. The history of morality not
only appears in judicial, religious, and philosophical treatises, but in
literature as well. In fact, drama is probably one of the best sources
for studying the evolution of social morality. The dramatists of the
Golden Age were Christian dialecticians interested in the propagation
of a given ethic, but who, as playwrights, also presented moral
dilemmas for their dramatic effect.

The approach to questions of morality in drama varies according to the individuality of the dramatist and the dominant beliefs of the time when the work is written. There was a general tendency in the baroque period in Spain to elevate poetry, allegory, and drama to ideal truth. The artist was thought to be a channel of revelation, and dramatists, when they treated the faith, often exercised the functions of a priest. However, dramatic art was not subordinated to religion and moral philosophy, nor were the Golden Age dramatists principally philosophers or moralists. Although they often included theological and philosophical homilies in their works, since the purpose of their drama was both to teach and to delight, their works were not primarily didactic as were the morality plays and the mysteries of the Middle Ages. What makes the Spanish dramatists seem more moralistic than those of other European countries is the unique way in which they employed the principle of poetic justice.[6] The guilty characters are punished and the good ones are rewarded according to the author's sense of justice, leaving nothing to chance. Besides being aesthetically pleasing, the drama was theological to the extent that moral warnings and poetic justice were included as essential conditions for the dramatic pleasure of the audiences in Spain. In order to comprehend the theme of a Golden Age play one must take into consideration the chain of causality of the action and the author's ethical view as revealed by his dramatization of the rightness and wrongness of human conduct. This ethical stance appears in the morality of the characters,[7] coincides with the sanction of poetic justice, and many times is an essential part of the main theme.

Since Thomistic natural-law ethics was vital to the climate of opinion of Golden Age Spain, it became an integral and important part of the drama. Related to the main themes of these plays are natural-law tenets, which are sometimes general, as in the case of *La mejor espigadera, El gran teatro del mundo*, and *A Dios por razón de estado*, and sometimes more specific, as in *Fuenteovejuna* and *No hay más fortuna que Dios*.

La mejor espigadera treats one of the most general principles of natural law—charity. Following Aristotle, Thomas thinks of society as a mutual exchange of services for the sake of the common good of the community. Central to this society is charity. In *La mejor espigadera* Tirso de Molina's treatment of Naomi, Boaz and Ruth illustrates the significance of charity and the communal spirit of man in society, as these exemplary characters fulfill their social obligation of brotherly love, bringing about metaphysical harmony between man and God.

The same general principle of charity is treated in *El gran teatro del mundo*. Here three laws are promulgated to man, the natural law, the written law and the law of grace; all incline man toward the supernatural good and oblige him to conform to the norm of morality. Man's purpose in life is to attain his last end and to help others attain theirs, following the natural law precepts *ama al otro como a ti* and *obra bien, que Dios es Dios*.

In contrast to the social aspects of natural law treated in *La mejor espigadera* and *El gran teatro del mundo*, the *auto sacramental A Dios por razón de estado* concerns itself with the relationship of man to God. Following Aquinas, Calderón demonstrates the concept that man can know God through his observance of the governance of things, and that this knowledge, perfected by written law and faith, obliges him to worship.

While the natural-law tenets in the preceding three plays are general, *Fuenteovejuna* and *No hay más fortuna que Dios* treat specific tenets which are arrived at by a more complicated process of reasoning. In *Fuenteovejuna* Lope de Vega demonstrates the principle that natural law gives man the right to pursue happiness in a peaceful and orderly manner and allows him to protect this right by all means which are not intrinsically wrong. The unjust ruler is considered by natural law to be more than a violator of human rights. He is rebelling against the divine system by which God rules the world. Thus when, in *Fuenteovejuna*, the Comendador becomes an unjust aggressor, resistance is morally correct.

The natural-law precepts concerning fortune and providence in *No hay más fortuna que Dios* are the most complex principles treated in this study. Basic to this play is the idea that there exists a highest good for which man strives. Here, as in *El gran teatro del mundo*, man does not fully understand the natural order, nor does he comprehend the significance of distributive justice. His erroneous judgment leads him, in his pursuit of happiness, to choose the apparent rather than the true good. He attributes effects to secondary causes rather than to God, the primary cause, and he worships the false deity fortune. Through natural reason the characters finally come to know that the only object which will fulfill their desires is God and that the only way in which they can find true happiness is through the possession of this highest good.

It is evident, then, that principles of Thomistic natural-law ethics play a vital role in the main themes of the plays discussed. These representative dramas illustrate the great impact that natural law had on the culture of Golden Age Spain. This study, through close textual analysis, has shown that knowledge of this doctrine is essential to the understanding of the central themes of five dramatic works of seventeenth-century Spain, and that an awareness of certain tenets of natural-law ethics assures an enriched comprehension of Golden Age drama.

Notes

Chapter 1

1. Carl L. Becker, *The Heavenly City of the Eighteenth-Century Philosophers* (New Haven, Conn., 1966), p. 5. Becker's primary interest is in the relationship of thirteenth-century rationalism to the French Enlightenment. However his conclusions seem to apply equally to the resurgence of Scholasticism in Spain of the Golden Age. See his thought-provoking chapter "Climates of Opinion," pp. 1-31.

2. The concept of the world as a drama can be traced to Greco-Latin antiquity and will be treated in the chapter on *El gran teatro del mundo*.

3. Becker, *Heavenly City*, p. 7.

4. Ibid., pp. 8-9.

5. For studies on Platonism in Spanish literature see Ludwig Pfandl, *Historia de la literatura nacional española en la edad de oro*, trans. Jorge Rubió Balaguer (Barcelona, 1952), pp. 32-42; and Otis H. Green, *Spain and the Western Tradition*, 4 vols. (Madison, Wis., 1963-66). See especially 3:307-12, of the latter.

6. Alexander A. Parker in an illuminating study argues convincingly that the picaresque novel was an answer to the literature of escapism. Treating the First Part of Mateo Alemán's *Guzmán de Alfarache* he says: "It satisfied the demands of the Counter-Reformation in that, being realistic, it was truthful and responsible. It served the ends of truth in that the story explicitly illustrated the doctrines of sin, repentance and salvation, the hero being one who, like Mary Magdalen, goes in search of the love of the world only to land in infamy, but who is able in his degradation to respond, like her, to the higher love. The heroes of romance are thus replaced by a picaroon—a thief, criminal, and galley-slave—who yet wins through to regeneration in the end.

"Only in this sense did the Spanish picaresque novel arise as a reaction to the romances—not as satire or parody, but as a deliberate alternative, a 'truthful' literature in response to the explicit demands of the Counter-Reformation." *Literature and the Delinquent* (Edinburgh, 1967), p. 22.

7. "An Introduction to the Ideology of the Baroque in Spain," *Symposium* 1 (1946):99.

8. For a study of Aristotelianism and its Christian, Moslem, and Jewish branches of Scholasticism see Julián Marías, *Historia de la filosofía* (Madrid, 1969), pp. 151-57, 160-70.

9. *Political Thought in Sixteenth-Century Spain* (Oxford, 1963), p. 11.

10. St. Thomas Aquinas, *Summa Theologica*, trans. English Dominican Fathers, 3 vols. (New York, 1947), 1-2, Q90, a1, meaning part 1 of part 2, question 90, article 1. Hereafter cited as *S. T.*

11. *S. T.*, 1-2, Q91, a1.
12. *S. T.*, 1-2, Q91, a2.
13. *S. T.*, 1-2, Q94, a2.
14. *S. T.*, 1-2, Q94, a6.
15. Becker, *Heavenly City*, pp. 33-70.
16. Aristotle, *On the Art of Poetry*, trans. Lane Cooper, rev. ed. (Ithaca, N.Y., 1962), pp. 9-10.
17. Ernst Curtius, *European Literature and the Latin Middle Ages*, trans. Willard R. Trask (New York, 1963), p. 478.
18. Horace, *On the Art of Poetry* in *Classical Literary Criticism*, trans. T. S. Dorsch (Baltimore, Md., 1967), pp. 90-91.
19. William Carlton McCrary, "The Classical Tradition in Spanish Dramatic Theory of the Sixteenth and Seventeenth Centuries" (Ph.D. diss., University of Wisconsin, 1958), pp. 33-36.

Chapter 2

1. Professors Spitzer, Wardropper, and McCrary have studied this work as it is related to the Platonic metaphysic of world harmony. Leo Spitzer, "A Central Theme and Its Structural Equivalent in Lope's *Fuenteovejuna*," *Hispanic Review* 23 (1955):274-92. Bruce Wardropper, *"Fuenteovejuna:* El gusto y lo justo," *Studies in Philology* 53 (1956):159-71. William C. McCrary, *"Fuenteovejuna:* Its Platonic Vision and Execution," *Studies in Philology* 58 (1961):179-91. I cannot agree that *Fuenteovejuna* is a political play as D. H. Roaten and F. Sánchez y Escribano imply, nor that it is a "plea for liberty," as Rudolph Schevill maintains. D. H. Roaten and F. Sánchez y Escribano, *Wölflin's Principles in Spanish Drama: 1500-1700* (New York, 1952), pp. 94-132. Rudolph Schevill, *The Dramatic Art of Lope de Vega* (Berkeley, 1918), pp. 113-15. I believe that Professor Casalduero is justified in taking issue with Menéndez Pelayo's attempt to read democracy into *Fuenteovejuna.* Joaquín Casalduero, *"Fuenteovejuna," Revista de Filología Hispánica* 5 (1943):21-44. Trans. by Ruth Whittredge as *"Fuenteovejuna:* Form and Meaning," *Tulane Drama Review* 4 (1959):83-107.
2. See C. E. Anibal, "The Historical Elements of Lope's *Fuenteovejuna*," *PMLA* 49 (1934):657-718.
3. Professor Wardropper remarks, *"Fuenteovejuna* to sum up, is a political play, but only in a very special sense. It examines relations between individuals—ethical life—and between social groups—political life. And it illustrates the connections between the two sets of relationships. Ethics and politics are shown to be inseparable. The two spheres of conduct are concentric." *"Fuenteovejuna,"* p. 171.
4. G. W. Ribbans, "The Meaning and Structure of Lope's *Fuenteovejuna*," *Bulletin of Hispanic Studies* 21 (1954):150-70. See also Albert S. Gérard, "Self-Love in Lope de Vega's *Fuenteovejuna* and Corneille's *Tite et Bérénice*," *Australian Journal of French Studies* 4 (1967):178.
5. For a discussion of poetic justice see Alexander A. Parker, *The Approach to the Spanish Drama of the Golden Age* (London, 1957), pp. 7-10.
6. Roy W. Battenhouse, *Marlowe's "Tamburlaine": A Study in Renaissance Moral Philosophy* (Nashville, Tenn., 1964), p. 148.
7. For Aquinas's views on free will see *S. T.*, 1, Q83, and for his treatise on man's last end with relation to free will see *S. T.*, 1-2, Q1, a1.

8. Battenhouse, *Marlowe's "Tamburlaine,"* p. 126.
9. Professors C. E. Anibal and Albert E. Sloman have failed to see the importance of the subplots in *Fuenteovejuna*. Anibal believes that the *Reyes Católicos* were "accorded attention quite out of proportion to their minor function in the drama," that they are a "distracting element." He marvels that the main plot (the rebellion) should be joined to a secondary plot (the Maestre's unsuccessful attack on Ciudad Real) so irrelevant (p. 657). Sloman is of the opinion that the secondary plot (the Ciudad Real episode) is linked to the main action in spirit but that though it provides emphasis, it is by no means essential to the play. "Indeed, with but minor alterations, the play could stand with the secondary action removed." "The Structure of Calderón's *La vida es sueño*," *Modern Language Review* 47 (1953):657.
10. McCrary, *"Fuenteovejuna,"* pp. 182–83.
11. Of course this does not preclude the Platonic influence in the play as perceived by Professors Spitzer, Wardropper, and McCrary.
12. *S. T.*, 2-2, Q42, a2.
13. Alexander A. Parker believes that treason and rape are dramatically unified in this play. "Reflections on a New Definition of Baroque Drama," *Bulletin of Hispanic Studies* 30 (1953):146.
14. Lope Félix de Vega Carpio, *Fuenteovejuna*, in *Obras escogidas*, ed. Federico Carlos Sainz de Robles, 2 vols. (Madrid, 1958), 1:840. Subsequent references to this play will be from this edition and page numbers will be parenthesized in the text.
15. For a historical view of the play see Anibal, "Historical Elements of *Fuenteovejuna*," pp. 657–718.
16. *S. T.*, 2-2, Q64.
17. St. Thomas Aquinas, *On Kingship*, trans. Gerald B. Phelan, 2 vols. (Toronto, 1949), bk.1, chaps. 7–15; and Francisco Suárez, *A Treatise on Laws and God the Lawgiver*, in *Selections from Three Works*, trans. Gwladys L. Williams, Ammi Brown, and John Waldron (Oxford, 1944), bk.2, chaps. 17–20.
18. Aquinas relies on Aristotle's *Politics* for his condemnation of tyranny in government. See *S. T.*, 2-2, Q42, a2.
19. McCrary, *"Fuenteovejuna,"* p. 191.
20. *S. T.*, 2-2, Q42, a2.
21. Treating the violence on the part of the villagers, Gérard says, "Already in *Fuenteovejuna*, it can be observed that the Christian dialectics of self-denial and self-fulfillment is transposed to the sphere of earthly experience. The conservative notion of total reliance on God is briefly expressed by the Mayor when he exclaims: ' ¡Justicia del cielo baje! ...' But this is merely an ephemeral stage in the inner development of the peasants, who soon realize that God's justice will not operate unless they deliberately turn themselves into its active instruments. And the selflessness of the villagers receives its due compensation on earth, leading as it does to the instauration of perfect concord in human society. It is one of the central ideas of the *comedia lopesca* that man has the power—and the duty—to change the *civitas terrena* into a genuine reflection of the *civitas caelestis* by observing, and if need be by enforcing observance of, God's law." "Self-Love," p. 197.

Chapter 3

1. There have been few published studies of Tirso's biblical plays. Among these, Edward Glaser deals with the characters of *La mejor espigadera* and their

relation to the biblical account in his penetrating study, *"La mejor espigadera,"* *Les Lettres Romanes* 14 (1960):199–218. Included in J. C. J. Metford's "Tirso de Molina's Old Testament Plays," *Bulletin of Hispanic Studies* 27 (1950): 149–63, is an examination of Tirso's dramatic technique in this play. I. L. McClelland mentions *La mejor espigadera* in "The Conception of the Supernatural in the Plays of Tirso de Molina," *Bulletin of Spanish Studies* 19 (1942):148–63.

2. Tirso does not hesitate to add the symbol of the Eucharist which was frequently represented in *autos* at this time. After giving food to the starving husband and wife, Naomi exclaims in a puzzled manner:

> ¡Qué la maldición de Adán,
> mi Dios, tenga tal poder
> que llegue en un padre a tanto
> que a quien dió la vida y ser,
> coma! Pero ¿qué me espanto
> si a Vos os han de comer?

The idea of cannibalism does not appear in the Book of Ruth and obviously has been added to increase the dramatic effect of the famine, Elimelech's avarice, and Naomi's magnanimity. Tirso de Molina, *La mejor espigadera*, in *Obras dramáticas completas*, ed. Blanca de los Ríos, 3 vols. (Madrid, 1946), 1:985. Subsequent references to this play will be from this edition, and page numbers will be parenthesized in the text.

3. For an examination of Tirso's fidelity to the Bible see J. C. J. Metford, "Tirso's Old Testament Plays," pp. 152–56.

4. In this play Tirso repeatedly refers to God as directing his creatures to their ends, thus expressing the necessary relation of the Creator to his creation, the eternal law or divine providence. For Thomas Aquinas the decree of God's will whereby creatures attain their ends is the eternal law. This law includes both the physical and the moral laws. Free beings are directed to their ends by moral law while those beings which are not free are directed by the physical laws inherent in their natures. Thomas holds that since God's very essence is eternal, the plan of his intellect and the decree of his will are also eternal. The eternal law as applied to creatures is the natural law. The rational creature's participation in the eternal law is natural law in the sense of natural moral law. See *S. T.*, 1-2, Q91, a1,2. For Aquinas's explanation of how natural law is promulgated to man through his reason see *S. T.*, 1-2, Q94, a6.

5. *S. T.*, 1-2, Q21, a1.

6. Aquinas argues that man cannot find happiness in material wealth. "It is impossible for man's happiness to consist in wealth. For wealth is twofold, as the Philosopher says (*Polit.* i. 3), viz., natural and artificial. Natural wealth is that which serves man as a remedy for his natural wants . . . while artificial wealth is that which is not a direct help to nature, as money, but is invented by the art of man, for the convenience of exchange, and as a measure of things salable.

"Now it is evident that man's happiness cannot consist in natural wealth. For wealth of this kind is sought for the sake of something else, viz., as a support of human nature: consequently it cannot be man's last end, rather is it ordained to man as to its end. . . .

"And as to artificial wealth, it is not sought save for the sake of natural wealth; since man would not seek it except because, by its means, he procures for himself the necessaries of life. Consequently much less can it be considered in the light of the last end. Therefore it is impossible for happiness, which is the last end of man, to consist in wealth." *S. T.*, 1-2, Q2, a1.

7. The peasants thank Naomi and prophesy her role with regard to the Messiah, thereby introducing the theme of divine providence. See p. 984.

8. Ruth is a good example of Thomas Aquinas's statement that "the rational creature is subject to Divine providence in the most excellent way, in so far as it itself partakes of a share of providence, by being provident both for itself and for others. Wherefore it has a share of the Eternal Reason, whereby it has a natural inclination to its proper act and end: and this participation of the eternal law in the rational creature is called the natural law." *S. T.,* 1-2, Q91, a2.

9. I. L. McClelland, in dealing with the supernatural elements related to *La mejor espigadera,* treats Naomi's prediction of Mahlon's bad end, but she does not mention the curses, blessings, and other prophecies, although they have the same dramatic effect that she attributes to Naomi's warning: "The warning— that only evil can ensue from deserting the true God—does not in itself, of course, constitute an omen. But it is from such logical forecasts as these that, in real life, the idea of the more elaborate fortune-telling properties associated with the supernatural develop; and Tirso, who was intuitively aware of this fact, devoted some of his less distracted moments to its demonstration." "The Conception of the Supernatural," p. 148.

10. See *S. T.*, 1-2, Q6–9, 12–17.

11. For Thomas Aquinas's treatment of the last end as the highest good for man, see *S. T.*, 1-2, Q1, a4,5.

12. Speaking of virtue Thomas says it is "a habit of choosing the mean appointed by reason as a prudent man would appoint it." *S. T.*, 1-2, Q59, a1.

13. The same peasants who condemned Elimelech for his avarice praise Boaz for his generosity, emphasizing the dramatic contrast between the two characters. The workers believe that the good crop stems from Boaz's goodness, and his charitable acts are interpreted as a basis for the harmony between God and man:

> GOMOR.   ¡ Oh Asael!
> Oraciones de Bohoz
> mos [*sic*] han dado el año lleno.
> HERBEL.   Es santo Bohoz.
> LISIS.   Es bueno.
>
> (1015)

14. *S. T.*, 1-2, Q61, a2.

15. For a discussion on charity in which Thomas combines love of God and of neighbor see *S. T.*, 1-2, QQ24–44, especially Q26.

Chapter 4

1. For the reader who wishes to consult a more complete study of Calderón's *autos sacramentales,* the best is Alexander A. Parker's *The Allegorical Drama of Calderón* (Oxford, 1943). By the same author, see also "The Chronology of Calderón's *autos sacramentales* from 1647," *Hispanic Review* 37 (1969):164–88. For a good study of the origin and development of the *auto sacramental,* including an investigation of the miracle, mystery, and morality

plays, see Bruce W. Wardropper, *Introducción al teatro religioso· del Siglo de Oro* (Madrid, 1953). See also Eugenio Frutos, *La filosofía de Calderón en sus autos sacramentales* (Zaragoza, 1952); Viola M. Dorsey, "The *Autos Sacramentales* of Calderón de la Barca" (Ph.D. diss., Stanford University, 1963); F. G. Very, *The Spanish Corpus Christi Procession* (Valencia, 1962); Lucy Elizabeth Weir, *The Ideas Embodied in the Religious Dramas of Calderón* (Lincoln, Nebr., 1940); N. D. Shergold and J. E. Varey, *Los autos sacramentales en Madrid en la época de Calderón 1637-1681* (Madrid, 1961).

2. For a historical view of the drama of the Middle Ages and the *auto sacramental* see N. D. Shergold, *A History of the Spanish Stage* (Oxford, 1967). A parallel treatment of French medieval drama which may prove of interest is W. L. Wiley, *The Early Public Theatre in France* (Cambridge, Mass., 1960).

3. Professor Parker believes that in the religious theater of the Spanish Renaissance the *auto sacramental* remained theocentric, continuing the tradition of the morality and mystery plays of the Middle Ages. "De sobra es sabido que el drama religioso medieval—misterios y moralidades—dejó de existir en Europa con el Renacimiento. El teatro dejó de ser teocéntrico para trocarse en antropocéntrico. Pero hubo un país que se negó a aceptar la nueva cultura en toda su integridad, y ese país fue España. . . . El arte renacentista español nunca dejó de ser teocéntrico." Alexander A. Parker, "Calderón, el dramaturgo de la escolástica," *Revista de estudios hispánicos*, no. 3 (1935), p. 275.

4. Pfandl, *Historia de la literatura nacional*, p. 474. See also Ignacio Escobar, "Teatro sacramental y existencial de Calderón de la Barca," *Cuadernos hispanoamericanos*, no. 134 (1961), pp. 222-23.

5. See J. E. Varey and N. D. Shergold, "La Tarasca de Madrid. Un aspecto de la procesión del Corpus durante los siglos XVII y XVIII," *Clavileño* 4 (1953), no. 20, pp. 18-26.

6. Bruce Wardropper cites Lope's definition of the *auto sacramental* as the first in existence.

> Y ¿qué son autos? —Comedias
> a honor y gloria del pan,
> que tan devota celebra
> esta coronada villa,
> porque su alabanza sea
> confusión de la herejía
> y gloria de la fe nuestra,
> todas de historias divinas.

Commenting on this definition, Wardropper says, "No hacía sino recordar uno de los resortes del drama sacramental de su niñez. . . . la lucha contra el luteranismo, que revestía cierta importancia en la época inmediatamente postridentina, perdió el sentido de urgencia cuando el peligro de la herejía se veía totalmente desarraigado de la España de la Contrarreforma." *Introducción al teatro religioso*, pp. 27-28.

7. Pedro Calderón de la Barca, *Obras completas,* ed. Ángel Valbuena Prat, 3 vols. (Madrid, 1969), 3:426-27.

8. Calderón, *Obras*, 3:42.

9. Ibid.

10. For a description of the staging of the *autos sacramentales*, with a good account of the plays performed in Madrid, the *carros*, and the protests against

the *autos*, see Hugo A. Rennert, *The Spanish Stage in the Time of Lope de Vega* (New York, 1909), pp. 297–321; Shergold, *History of the Spanish Stage*, pp. 426–36, 486–94; N. D. Shergold and J. E. Varey, "A Problem in the Staging of *Autos Sacramentales* in Madrid 1647–1648," *Hispanic Review* 32 (1964):12–35; Ludwig Pfandl, *Cultura y costumbres del pueblo español de los siglos XVI y XVII*, trans. Félix García (Barcelona, 1959), pp. 235–39.

11. In 1662, the inquisition condemned Calderón's *Las órdenes militares* for its treatment of the Immaculate Conception. The *auto* was withdrawn, later rewritten, and performed in 1671. See J. E. Varey and N. D. Shergold, "Datos históricos sobre los primeros teatros de Madrid: prohibiciones de autos y comedias y sus consecuencias (1644-1651)," *Bulletin Hispanique* 62 (1960): 286–325. Also see William J. Entwistle, "La controversia en los autos de Calderón," *Nueva Revista de Filología Hispánica* 2 (1948):223–38.

12. Parker, *Allegorical Drama*, pp. 20, 24.

13. For a study of the fate of the *autos* in the eighteenth century, see Giuseppi Rossi, "Calderón nella polemica settecentesca sugli *autos sacramentales,"* *Studi Mediolatini e volgari* 1 (1953):197–224, and Ramón Esquer Torres, "Las prohibiciones de comedias y autos sacramentales en el siglo XVIII," *Segismundo*, no. 2 (1965), pp. 1–40.

14. "The Religious Dramas of Calderón," *Liverpool Studies* 2 (1946): 121–22.

15. Bruce W. Wardropper, "Menéndez Pelayo on Calderón," *Criticism* 7 (1965):363.

16. Ibid., p. 372.

17. Ibid., p. 366. Although he does not treat the *autos* specifically, Albert E. Sloman merits mention for his book *The Dramatic Craftsmanship of Calderón* (Oxford, 1958). Wardropper's introduction to his collection *Critical Essays on the Theatre of Calderón* (New York, 1965), comments on the contributions of some German and American scholars to Calderonian scholarship, and also mentions the work of Ángel Valbuena Prat (pp. vii–xiii).

18. Parker, *Allegorical Drama*, pp. 59–60. Referring to the use of the Eucharist as a theme in the *autos*, Ángel Valbuena Prat says: "Dentro de los autos teológicos ocupa un lugar aparte *La hidalga del valle*, citada, por no referirse para nada al Sacramento, ni haberse representado en fiestas del Corpus, pero en él la trama alegórica es igual que las de las piezas eucarísticas." *Historia de la literatura española* (Barcelona, 1953), 2:515.

19. Parker, *Allegorical Drama*, p. 60.

20. Nicolaus Margraff has produced an index which lists specific references to the Bible, the Church Fathers, and the Scholastics, indicating the verses of the *autos* where they are to be found. *Der Mensch und sein Seelenleben in den Autos Sacramentales des Don Pedro Calderón de la Barca* (Bonn, 1912), pp. 101–02.

21. Pedro Calderón de la Barca, *Sueños hay que verdad son*, in *Obras*, 3:1215.

22. Pedro Calderón de la Barca, *Las órdenes militares*, in *Obras*, 3:1019.

23. See *S. T.*, 1, Q78, a4-8, and Etienne H. Gilson, *The Philosophy of St. Thomas Aquinas*, trans. Edward Bullough (St. Louis, 1937), pp. 221–32.

24. Parker, *Allegorical Drama*, p. 75.

25. Ibid., p. 81.

26. See Lucien-Paul Thomas, "Les jeux de scène et l'architecture des idées dans Calderón," in *Homenaje ofrecido a Menéndez Pidal* (Madrid, 1925),

2:503–30, and "François Bertaut et les conceptions de Calderón," *Revue de Littérature Comparée* 4 (1924): 199–221.

27. Margraff supports his view by citing the abundance of Augustinian references found in the *autos. Mensch und sein Seelenleben,* p. 60.

28. "While the framework of his ideas is Augustinian and Franciscan, the details are invariably filled in with a purely Thomistic terminology and technique. When analysing moral conflicts it is nearly always to St. Thomas that he goes for the precise roles which the reason and the will must play, and for exact definitions of the virtues and the vices." Parker, *Allegorical Drama,* p. 70. Eugenio Frutos counters Margraff's exaggeration of Augustinian influence by citing specific references to Thomas Aquinas. *La filosofía de Calderón,* pp. 76–77. See also Ángel Valbuena Prat, *Calderón, su personalidad, su arte dramático, su estilo, y sus obras* (Barcelona, 1941), p. 60.

29. "Los autos sacramentales son el género más apropiado para la síntesis de la doctrina católica. Calderón, en ellos, sigue tanto la parte expositiva de los teólogos como la argumentación y construcción de la escolástica, ya, directamente, a base de la *Summa Theologica* de Santo Tomás, ya según los jesuítas españoles del final del siglo XVI, como Suárez." Ángel Valbuena Prat, ed. *Autos Sacramentales,* by Pedro Calderón de la Barca, Clásicos Castellanos (Madrid, 1967), 1:xxviii–xxix.

30. Parker, *Allegorical Drama,* p. 70.

Chapter 5

1. Jutta Wille studies the moral problem in *El gran teatro del mundo* and *A tu prójimo como a ti,* relating it to Christian ethics. *Calderóns Spiel Der Erlösung* (Munich, 1932), pp. 25–26.

2. Antonio Vilanova has traced the theme of the world as a theater back to Greco-Latin antiquity in "El tema del gran teatro del mundo," *Boletín de la Real Academia de Buenas Letras de Barcelona* 23 (1950):153–88. Of special interest in Seneca's *Epistle* 77 in which the idea that life is a drama is joined to the recognition of the brevity of human existence; since man must face the imminence of death, he ought to subject his existence to a moral code of conduct. As in Calderón's treatment of the world as a stage, it is demonstrated that the pompousness and pride of the world do not represent felicity, because they are nothing but transitory disguises which are soon to end. In Vilanova's study of the Stoics and their examination of this theme he says, "Es evidente que la adaptación de la filosofía del estoicismo a las creencias cristianas, trae consigo la identificación del autor de la comedia con Dios mismo, que es quien nos asigna el papel que nos toca representar en el gran teatro del mundo" (p. 155). The idea of life as a drama, as treated by Desiderius Erasmus (*The Praise of Folly,* trans. Hoyt Hopewell [Princeton, 1941], p. 37) and as found in the Jesuit drama of Calderón's time (Parker, *Allegorical Drama,* pp. 110–11) influenced much of Spanish literature of the sixteenth and seventeenth centuries. Some examples of the use of this theme in the Golden Age are: Juan Huarte de San Juan in the *Proemio* to his *Examen de Ingenios,* Biblioteca de autores españoles, no. 65 (Madrid, 1953), p. 407; Mateo Alemán, *Guzmán de Alfarache,* ed. Samuel Gili Gaya, 5 vols. (Madrid, 1962), 2:151; Miguel de Cervantes Saavedra, *Don Quijote,* in *Obras completas,* ed. Ángel Valbuena Prat (Madrid, 1960), pp. 1309–10. For a more detailed study of this idea in Spanish literature, see Ángel Valbuena Prat, *Historia del teatro español* (Barcelona, 1956), pp. 365–89 and Vilanova, pp. 159–86.

3. Parker, *Allegorical Drama*, p. 113.
4. *Historia del teatro*, pp. 370-71.
5. *S. T.*, 1-2, Q1, a8.
6. *S. T.*, 1, Q78, a3.
7. *S. T.*, 1-2, Q95, a4.
8. *S. T.*, 1-2, Q110, a2,3.
9. "Law is a rule and measure of acts, whereby man is induced to act or is restrained from acting: for *lex* (law) is derived from *ligare* (to bind), because it binds one to act. Now the rule and measure of human acts is the reason, which is the first principle of human acts . . . since it belongs to the reason to direct to the end, which is the first principle in all matters of action, according to the Philosopher (*Phys.*, ii). Now that which is the principle in any genus, is the rule and measure of that genus: for instance, unity in the genus of numbers, and the first movement in the genus of movements. Consequently it follows that law is something pertaining to reason." *S. T.*, 1-2, Q90, a1.
10. *S. T.*, 1-2, Q90, a4.

11.   *Dos puertas: la una es la cuna*
             y la otra es el sepulcro.
             Y para que no les falten
             las galas y adornos juntos,
             para vestir los papeles
             tendré prevenido a punto
             al que hubiere de hacer rey,
             púrpura y laurel augusto;
             al valiente capitán,
             armas, valores y triunfos;
             . . . .
             Al religioso, obediencias;
             al noble le daré honras,
             y libertades al vulgo.
             Al labrador, que a la tierra
             ha de hacer fértil a puro
             afán, por culpa de un necio,
             le daré instrumentos rudos.
             A la que hubiere de hacer
             la dama, le daré sumo
             adorno en las perfecciones,
             dulce veneno de muchos.
                              (206-07)

12. Bernice Hamilton, *Political Thought in Sixteenth-Century Spain* (Oxford, 1963), pp. 12-16.
13. *S. T.*, 1-2, Q91, a2.
14. *S. T.*, 1-2, Q21, a1.
15. In regard to these commands Parker says: "Love and praise of God is not possible in isolation, it implies love of one's neighbour. Neither the individual nor society can achieve the ends for which they exist unless human actions are infused by this twofold yet unified love of charity. In the actual performance of the play these two aspects are kept distinct. Each actor will be required to show in successive scenes whether his attitude to life in general and

to his neighbour in particular is determined and directed by charity."
Allegorical Drama, p. 129.

16. The interesting social problem that el Labrador presents is analyzed by Ángel Valbuena Prat, who believes that the character represents a satire of the customs of Calderón's times (*Historia del teatro*, pp. 371–73). Parker describes el Labrador as gross, ungracious, churlish and revengeful (*Allegorical Drama*, pp. 131–35). Sturgis E. Leavitt claims that el Labrador is a "chronic but humorous grumbler" who was meant to be not only an amusing character, but one entirely sympathetic to the audience. "Humor in the *Autos* of Calderón," *Hispania* 39 (1956):143.

Chapter 6

1. *S. T.*, 1, Q103, a7.
2. *S. T.*, 1, Q19, a8.
3. *S. T.*, 1, Q22, a4.
4. *S. T.*, 1, Q116, a3.
5. Thomas Aquinas explains this principle of finality:

Every agent, of necessity, acts for an end. For if, in a number of causes ordained to one another, the first be removed, the others must, of necessity, be removed also. Now the first of all causes is the final cause. The reason of which is that matter does not receive form, save in so far as it is moved by an agent; for nothing reduces itself from potentiality to act. But an agent does not move except out of intention for an end. For if the agent were not determinate to some particular effect, it would not do one thing rather than another: consequently in order that it produce a determinate effect, it must, of necessity, be determined to some certain one, which has the nature of an end. . . . it is proper to the rational nature to tend to an end, as directing (agens) and leading itself to the end: whereas it is proper to the irrational nature to tend to an end, as directed or led by another. (*S. T.*, 1-2, Q1, a2)

6. *S. T.*, 1-2, Q1, a4. Aquinas is basing his theory on Aristotle's argument that there cannot be an infinitude of causes in movement, because there would then be no first mover. See Aristotle, *Physics*, bk. 8, chap. 5.

7. Concerning the end of good, Thomas elaborates on Augustine's statement: "Hence Augustine (*De Civ. Dei* xix. 1): 'In speaking of the end of good we mean now, not that it passes away so as to be no more, but that it is perfected so as to be complete.' It is therefore necessary for the last end so to fill man's appetite, that nothing is left besides it for man to desire. Which is not possible, if something else be required for his perfection. Consequently it is not possible for the appetite so to tend to two things, as though each were its perfect good." *S. T.*, 1-2, Q1, a5.

8. See Parker, "The Theology of the Devil in the Drama of Calderón," The Aquinas Society of London, Aquinas Paper, no. 32 (1958), p. 20.

9. Parker believes that Calderón goes to Thomas for the argument that original sin was an infinite fault because it offended God. Calderón holds that because of man's rejection of an *infinito objeto*, he has committed an *infinito delito*. See Pedro Calderón de la Barca, *No hay más fortuna que Dios*, ed. Alexander A. Parker (Manchester, 1962), p. 58.

10. Pedro Calderón de la Barca, *No hay más fortuna que Dios,* in *Obras,* ed. Ángel Valbuena Prat, 3 vols. (Madrid, 1969), 3:615. Subsequent references to Calderón's *autos sacramentales* will be from this edition, and page numbers will be parenthesized in the text.

11. For a study of la Discreción and its meaning in *No hay más fortuna que Dios,* see Parker, "The Meaning of *Discreción* in *No hay más fortuna que Dios:* The Medieval Background and Sixteenth- and Seventeenth-Century Usage," in his edition of Calderón, *No hay más fortuna,* pp. 77–92. Professor Parker points out the distinction between discretion and prudence. For Calderón, discretion is not a supernatural virtue like prudence; it is instead a natural virtue, "pointing to the perfection of the intellect that men can attain to by their own efforts, and leading them to the natural wisdom that is the threshold of supernatural life into which men can step with the aid of faith and grace" (p. 90). Discretion serves as the discursive element of reason, comparing one impression to another and coming to a conclusion as to what benefits the human being. The *Diccionario de Autoridades* defines *discreción* as the faculty which has as its function to know what is beneficial or harmful in the sensible order.

12. *S. T.,* 1, Q48,49.

13. Étienne H. Gilson, *The Christian Philosophy of St. Thomas Aquinas,* trans. L. K. Shook (New York, 1956), p. 156.

14. Ibid., pp. 156–59.

15. Parker, in Calderón, *No hay más fortuna,* pp. xx–xxi.

16. Thomas's argument for God as the first cause stems from his premise that there is an order of efficient cause and effect, that certain beings cause other beings to exist. Thomas argues that it is inconceivable that a limited being should be its own efficient cause since it would have first to exist in order to cause itself to exist. It needs another cause. He believes that it is not possible to proceed to infinity in a series of existentially subordinated efficient causes, and holds that if cause were removed the effect would cease. Hence, for Thomas if there were no first cause, there would be no present effect. See *S. T.,* 1, Q2, a3 and above p. 87 in text.

17. See *S. T.,* 1-2, Q91, a1.

18. See *S. T.,* 1-2, Q91, a2.

Chapter 7

1. Ángel Valbuena Prat, ed., *Obras completas,* by Pedro Calderón de la Barca, 3 vols. (Madrid, 1969), 3:32–33. Valbuena gives his critical opinion of *A Dios por razón de estado* in his *Nota preliminar* to the *auto:* "El desarrollo de la obra está bien, y es, hasta cierto punto interesante su trama. Como toda obra exclusivamente teológica y escolástica, se hace cansada." He includes his observation on Menéndez y Pelayo's commentary concerning this play: "En *Calderón y su teatro* (conferencia 3ª) sintetiza observaciones de Pedroso y añade otras agudas de su propia cosecha. Es quizá lo mejor que se ha escrito, en ese tiempo, sobre los autos; pero adolece de graves defectos: prejuicio contra el género, incomprensión del valor de la alegoría en el teatro y, lo peor, desconocimiento del tema mismo. Basta leer todos los autos y el estudio de Menéndez y Pelayo para dudar de que el escritor que ha removido la crítica sobre Calderón haya leído todas las obras de éste" (p. 849).

2. Pfandl, *Historia de la literatura*, p. 13.

3. *"Pensar.* Imaginar o rebolver alguna cosa en su memoria.... Pensamiento, la consideración de alguna cosa, *latine cogitativo.*" Sebastián de Covarrubias, *Tesoro de la lengua castellana o española* (1611), ed. Martín de Riquer (Barcelona, 1943). Also: *"Pensamiento.* Facultad o potencia imaginativa. *Lat. Mens. animi sensus. Vis imaginativa.* Se entiende tambien por el acto de entendimiento, con que imagina, considera o piensa en alguna cosa." *Diccionario de Autoridades* (1726; facsimile ed., Madrid, 1963). Covarrubias's definition of *ingenio* is "Una fuerça natural de entendimiento, investigadora de lo que por razón y discurso se puede alcançar en todo género de ciencias...." *Tesoro de la lengua.* Similarly, "Ingenio o potencia en el hombre, con que sutilmente discurre o inventa trazas, modos, machinas, y artificios o razones y argumentos, o percibe y aprehende facilmente las ciencias." *Autoridades.*

4. *S. T.,* 1, Q78, a4. Also see Étienne H. Gilson, *The Christian Philosophy of St. Thomas Aquinas,* pp. 200-222.

5. *S. T.,* 2-2, Q81, a1.

6. *S. T.,* 1, Q2, a3.

7. Aristotle, *Nichomachean Ethics,* bk. 2, chap. 12, 1162a, in *The Basic Works of Aristotle,* ed. Richard McKeon (New York, 1968).

8. "Matrimony is natural, because natural reason inclines thereto in two ways. First, in relation to the principal end of matrimony, namely the good of the offspring. For nature intends not only the begetting of offspring, but also its education and development until it reach the perfect state of man as man, and that is the state of virtue. Hence, according to the Philosopher (*Ethic.* viii. 11,12), we derive three things from our parents, namely *existence, nourishment,* and *education.* Now a child cannot be brought up and instructed unless it have certain and definite parents, and this would not be the case unless there were a tie between the man and a definite woman, and it is in this that matrimony consists." *S. T.,* 3, supp., Q41, a1.

9. "But Saul, still breathing threats and murder against the disciples of the Lord, went to the high priest and asked him for letters to the synagogues at Damascus, so that if he found any belonging to the Way, men or women, he might bring them bound to Jerusalem." Acts 9:1-2.

10. "Besides the natural and the human law it was necessary for the directing of human conduct to have a Divine law. And this for four reasons. First, because it is by law that man is directed how to perform his proper acts in view of his last end. And indeed if man were ordained to no other end than that which is proportionate to his natural faculty, there would be no need for man to have any further direction on the part of his reason, besides the natural law and human law which is derived from it. But since man is ordained to an end of eternal happiness which is inproportionate to man's natural faculty... it was necessary that, besides the natural and the human law, man should be directed to his end by a law given by God." *S. T.,* 1-2, Q91, a4.

11. *S. T.,* 1, Q2, a3.

Chapter 8

1. Francisco Bances Candamo, *Theatro de los theatros de los passados y presentes siglos,* ed. Duncan W. Moir (London, 1970), p. 80.

2. "Of literature it can be said that the grandest thoughts and the grandest feelings are to be found in the same works, and of drama it can be said that it

Notes to Pages 98-100   115

is not only more emotional than the current notion of it but also more intellectual. Great drama has occurred only sporadically in history, and historians have often shown that a new wave of drama rolls in on a new wave of vitality. The vitality is intellectual as much as it is anything else. Great drama generally rolls in on an idea, that idea being the informing thought of a new movement in history, a new image of man." Eric Bentley, *The Life of the Drama* (New York, 1964), p. 113.

3. Ibid., p. 114.

4. Referring to the relationship of ideas of an age to drama Bentley states: "If what I am saying is correct . . . the vitality of any drama that *is* vital would be in part intellectual, and . . . we would find the ideas of the age contributing to the life of any significant drama whatsoever. . . . Once intellect is seen as a potentially vitalizing thing, this body of work can also be seen as vital. I am thinking of medieval drama; the drama of the Golden Century in Spain; the German classics of the eighteenth century; and the modern 'drama since Ibsen.' " Ibid., p. 116. Bentley is a firm believer of the vitality and universality of drama as a genre. The Spanish Golden Age scholar must not overlook, however, the uniqueness of the *comedia*. See *Hispanic Review* 38 (1970), where the polemic of the universality versus the uniqueness of the *comedia* is treated by Eric Bentley in "Universality of the *Comedia*," pp. 147–62, and by Arnold G. Reichenberger in "The Uniqueness of the *Comedia*," pp. 163–73.

5. Bentley, *Life of the Drama*, p. 117.

6. A. A. Parker believes that, "The insistence on poetic justice can. . . make the Spanish drama offend against traditional dramatic theory by blurring the classical distinction between tragedy and comedy." *The Approach to the Spanish Drama of the Golden Age* (London, 1957), p. 8, also published in *Tulane Drama Review* 4 (1959):42–59. R. F. D. Pring-Mill differs to some extent with Parker's views of poetic justice in his introduction to *Lope de Vega (Five Plays)*, trans. Jill Booty (New York, 1961), pp. xviii, xxxi. In response to Professor Pring-Mill's comments Parker elaborates on his previous interpretation of poetic justice in "Towards a Definition of Calderonian Tragedy," *Bulletin of Hispanic Studies* 39 (1962):225–26.

7. "The imitation, which is also an action, must be carried on by agents, the *dramatis personae*. And these agents must necessarily be endowed by the poet with certain distinctive qualities both of Moral Character (*ethos*) and Intellect (*dianoia*)—one might say, of heart and head; for it is from a man's moral bent, and from the way in which he reasons, that we are led to ascribe goodness or badness, success or failure, to his acts. Thus, as there are two natural causes, moral bent and thought, of the particular deeds of men, so there are the same two natural causes of their success or failure in life. And the tragic poet must take cognizance of this." Aristotle, *On the Art of Poetry*, trans. Lane Cooper, rev. ed. (Ithaca, New York, 1962), p. 22.

Index

Acts of the Apostles, 79, 80, 82, 114
n.9
Alemán, Mateo, 103; on the world as
theater, 110 n.2
Allegory: in drama, 65-66; of world as
theater, 48-50, 53, 55. *See also Auto
sacramental*
Aníbal, C. E., 104 n.2, 105 n.9
Aquinas, Thomas. *See* Thomas Aquinas, Saint
Aratus of Soli, 82
Areopagus, 81, 82
Aristotle: and empiricism, 6; on law,
111 n.6; on marriage, 114 n.8; *Poetics*,
10-11, 114 n.7; *Politics*, 20, 105
n.18; on first mover, 112 n.6; on
society, 100; on tyranny, 21; on
wealth, 106 n.6
Atheism as a dramatic character,
89-90
Athens, 81-82
Augustine, 45, 79; *credo ut intelligam*,
10; on good, 112 n.7; philosophy of,
6; on truth, 9
Authority: of God, 60; of man, 60-61
Auto da fe, 5
Autor, 39
Auto sacramental: allegory in, 40,
43-45; and the climate of opinion,
5; and the Corpus Christi feast,
38-39; critics of, 41-42, 108 n.10,
109 n.11, n.13; definition of,
39-40; didactic, 99; and the Eucharist, 43, 109 n.18; and the Inquisition, 109 n.11; natural law in,
38; relation to liturgical drama, 38;
scholastic philosophy in, 45-46;
staging of, 41, 108 n.10
Averroës, 3
Averroists, 97

Bances Candamo, Francisco, 98
Battenhouse, Roy W., 104 n.6, 105 n.8
Becker, Carl: on the French Enlightenment, 103 n.1; on natural law
philosophy, 1-2; on the thirteenth
century, 2-3
Being: absence of, 70; and good, 8
Bentley, Eric: on drama as intellectual,
99; on Golden Age drama, 115 n.4;
on ideas in drama, 115 n.2
Bertaut, François: on Calderón, 110
n.7
Bible: and the *autos*, 38, 43; Calderón's use of, 33, 79, 80, 92, 94, 95,
97; Tirso's use of, 23-25, 105 n.1
Blameless self-defense, 20-21

Calderón de la Barca, Pedro: and the
autos, 12, 13; use of philosophy, 79,
101; use of theology, 79
Cano, Melchor, 7
Casalduero, Joaquín, 104 n.1
Cascales, Francisco de, 12
Cause: of causes, 86-87; contingent,
31, 60; and effect, 87; efficient, 77,
87; and order of cause and effect,
113 n.16; secondary, 64. *See also*
First cause
Central sense, 81
Cervantes, Miguel de: on the world as
theater, 110 n.2
Charity: concept of, 35; obligation of,
36, 56; represented in drama, 24-25,
27-30, 50-56, 58, 100-101; as a
virtue, 35, 55
Charles V (king of Spain), 5
Chastity as a good equivalent to life,
17, 20
Climate of opinion: Becker on, 1, 2, 5;
in Spain, 2, 5, 100, 102